Aleksei Sergeyevich Mazurin:
Easter. (From the archives of
the Russian Photographic
Society. Historical Museum,
Moscow.) Moscow, c. 1900.

A Portrait of Tsarist Russia

Unknown Photographs from the Soviet Archives

WITH TEXT BY
Y BARCHATOVA, T SABUROVA, G MIROLUBOVA, T PETROVA,
E NORKUTE, T SHIPOVA, A GOLOVINA, A YUSKIN

TRANSLATED FROM THE GERMAN BY MICHAEL ROBINSON

PANTHEON BOOKS

NEW YORK

Front cover: Otto Kirchner: Novo Devitshi Nunnery, Moscow, 11. September 1902.

Backcover: Anonymous: Back yard on the Wyborg-side of St Petersburg. Poor people, workers and small traders lived here. 1910.

*Endpaper
St Petersburg decorated for its two-hundredth birthday (see also rear endpaper).*

Library of Congress Cataloging-in-Publication Data

A Portrait of Tsarist Russia: unknown photographs from the Soviet Archives/by Y Barchatova ... [et al.].
    p.   cm.
1. Soviet Union—Description and travel—Views. 2. Soviet Union Biography—Portraits. 3. Soviet Union—History—19th century—Pictorial works. 4. Soviet Union—Social life and customs—1533–1917—Pictorial works. I Barchatova, Y.
DK 18.5.P67   1989
ISBN 0-394-58031-1
947-dc20   89-42685

Photographs copyright © 1989 by Planeta Publishers, Moscow.
English translation copyright © 1989 by Verlag Dirk Nishen. Selection of photographs and layout copyright © 1989 by Verlag Dirk Nishen, Am Tempelhofer Berg 6, 1000 Berlin 61.

Type: Walbaum Standard by Berthold, typeset by Nagel Fototype, Berlin. Reproduction by O. R. T. Kirchner + Graser, Berlin. Printed on 135 g double-coated offset paper by H. Heenemann, Berlin. Bound at Lüderitz & Bauer, Berlin.
The publishers would like to express their thanks to all the people involved with this project.
Printed in the Federal Republic of Germany.
First American Edition

Publisher's Note

The photos compiled in this volume have been reproduced from transparencies, which were placed at the publisher's disposal by the various contributing archives. With the exception of some of the photographs appearing in the margins and the double-page spreads, the photographs are reproduced without cropping. Unfortunately, the size and nature of the original photographs could not be determined in every case.

The publishers would like to thank their colleagues at Planeta Publishers, Moscow, for their cooperation in this unique publishing project: this book is published simultaneously in Germany, the United States, and Great Britain, and shortly thereafter in France, Italy, and the Soviet Union; different production routines created a variety of problems, and it was only Planeta's willingness to work together in solving them that made this production possible. A special thank you to Vladimir Seredin.

The publishers also thank the boards of trustees of the museums for their help with each new request and inquiry. We hope that this book will mark the beginning of a new kind of cooperation among an international group of photographic archives.

Contents

Yelena V Barchatova — Introduction — 7

Tatyana Saburova — Reminders of Russian History
The archive of the STATE HISTORY MUSEUM, Moscow — 38

Yelena V Barchatova — Everyday Pictures for Every Day
The archive of the SALTYKOV-SHCHEDRIN STATE
PUBLIC LIBRARY, Leningrad — 74

Galina A Mirolubova
Tatyana A Petrova — The Golden Age of Photography
The collection of the
HERMITAGE STATE MUSEUM, Leningrad — 100

Ebba Norkute — The Photographer and his Majesty
the Theater
The collection of the
STATE MUSEUM FOR THEATER AND MUSIC, Leningrad — 132

Tatyana Shipova — "A Memory for the Future"
The archive of the STATE LITERATURE MUSEUM, Moscow — 146

Alexandra Golovina — Preserved for Posterity
The collection of the STATE CENTRAL ARCHIVE OF
FILM AND PHOTOGRAPHIC DOCUMENTARY, Leningrad — 170

Albert G Yuskin — The Unforgettable Shape of Russia
The CENTRAL STATE ARCHIVE FOR RUSSIAN
FILM AND PHOTOGRAPHY, Krasnogorsk — 212

Photographic Processes — 254

Bibliography — 257

Index of Names — 258

*Anonymous: Vladimir Sta-
sov with his children. An un-
usually fine portrait of this
grand old man of Russian
photography. St Petersburg (?),
1903/1904.*

Introduction

Yelena V Barchatova

The photographs in this volume are drawn from seven different archives, and represent only a fraction of the material available. The present volume is intended simply as an introduction to Russian photography; we hope there will be more to come. This section is intended to introduce you to the photographers themselves, and to the institutions and periodicals devoted to photography in the first hundred years of its existence in Russia. If you are overwhelmed by the mass of information, why not turn to the photographs from time to time, just to get your second wind.

You will come across numerous names and dates again in the introductions to individual chapters. Photographs by Levitsky, Denier, and the elder Bulla, to give just three examples, are found in several archives. Nonetheless, we have decided not to arrange the material by photographer or by place, but to work largely chronologically within the individual archives. Thus repetition of certain names in different chapters does not mean repetition of material, and certainly not tedium, as the sympathetic reader will be swift to realize. Please use the index of names at the end of the book as a guide.

Russian photographers and scholars took a first look back at the way things had developed about fifty years after photography was discovered. The first purely photographic exhibition in Russia was held in St Petersburg in 1888. Its organizers compared the importance of photography with two other major inventions of the nineteenth century: in the early years steam had a tremendous effect on social development, while the second half of the century was dominated by electricity and photography. As Russia's first photographic magazine, *Photographic Art (Svetopis)*, pointed out, "Photography enjoyed an astonishing degree of success, one triumph following another with all the extraordinary speed which is the hallmark of our busy century."

The early exponents of Russian photography thought that it had a great contribution to make to the development of human civilization. They also recognized the twin qualities inherent in Louis Jacques Mandé Daguerre's invention: Florenti Pavlenkov, a distinguished publisher, called photography a "perfect violin, brought into being by an organic process involving chemistry and the heart, optics and emotion, apparatus and thought."

The RUSSIAN ACADEMY OF SCIENCE paid keen attention to scientific developments abroad, especially in Europe. Information about the discovery of photography was supplied at a very early stage by a corresponding member called Hammel. In the course of his travels in Europe in 1839 he acquired details of William Henry Fox Talbot's methods and the Daguerre process. The ACADEMY OF SCIENCE commissioned a chemist called Fritsche to conduct research into the photographic process known as the talbotype, which Talbot himself also called calotype (from *kalos*, Greek for "beautiful"). Early in

DECEMBRISTS
The Decembrists were participants in a failed military putsch against the autocracy of the Tsar on 26 December 1825 in St Petersburg. They were young guards officers who had become enthusiastic about ideas of liberal reform during their stay in Western Europe at the time of the wars of liberation. They were organized in two secret federations from 1822. Both groups were driven by a strong feeling of Greater Russian nationalism; one was in favor of a constitutional monarchy, the other preferred a centralist republic. They saw an opportunity to strike in the short-lived interregnum after the death of Alexander II (1 December 1825). The operation badly prepared was quickly defeated, especially as it met with little sympathy from Russian society. About 600 were brought to book, and 121 sentenced. Of these 5 were executed, and most of the rest sent to do forced labor in Siberia. The survivors were not pardoned until 1856.

TSAR NICHOLAS I (1825–1855)
After the Decembrist up-
rising the new Tsar Nicholas I
(1825–1855) reorganized the
Russian police, formed the
notorious "Third Section" of
His Majesty's Chancellery,
and created the gendarmerie
as a special permanent police
force. The great danger, as
the Decembrist uprising had
shown, was presented by
thoughts that led to deeds,
and so the "Third Section"
was set up as a sort of
thought police.
The gendarme was the con-
stantly present symbol of the
police state, and together
with the Orthodox priest became a hated symbol of reaction.
Under Nicholas I there were
556 outbreaks of unrest
among the peasants involving a parish or larger areas.

Nikolai Vassilyevich Gogol
(1809–1852). One of the
greatest prose writers and
humanists. His work is full of
religious and ethical themes
which mingle to create sympathy for all human beings,
an approach which was to
become characteristic of
Russian realism. The Over-
coat, the last of the five
St Petersburg novellas, is
considered to be the starting
point for "social sympathy"
in Russian literature.

1839 Fritsche delivered his report on heliogra-
phic experiments to the Academy. He based his
own work on leaf photograms produced by the
talbotype method, which he had succeeded in
improving. This was the first piece of Russian
research aimed at perfecting a photographic
process and using light to produce images. In
the autumn of 1838 one of the earliest daguerreotypes appeared in Russia—Colonel Temerin
took a picture of the Isaac Cathedral in St Petersburg, which was under construction at the
time, using a 25-minute exposure.

Photography and the Written Word

It was inevitable that discussions about the new
medium should begin to appear in writing. The
first item in the bibliography of Russian photographic literature was a brochure called *The Art
of Producing a Faithful Image in the Shortest
Possible Time, and Most Safely and Easily, of
Plans, Drawings, Maps, Plants, Ornaments,
and Silhouettes*, published in Moscow. The
wordiness of the title of this and other works
show how concerned writers were to convey
every possibility offered by the new medium to
their readers. In fact this particular article had
no direct connection with photography; it was a
report on a method of copying any illustration
through thin glass, using a paintbrush. Two
brochures directly concerned with images produced by light were *Light Images Produced by
the Method of Messrs Talbot and Lyassen or the
Daguerreotype Itself in Its Simplest Form* and
*A Description of the Practical Application of
Proper Daguerreotypy*.
The names of the authors of these early practical introductions to photography in Russian are
unknown. However, Aleksei Fyodorovich Grekov, an engraver and inventor, is thought to be
the author of another work entitled *Painter
without Paintbrush or Paint, Who Reproduces
Any Kind of Illustration, Portrait, Landscape,
etc., in Their Proper Color, Capturing Every
Nuance, in a Few Minutes*. A few months after
the invention of the daguerreotype, Grekov,
who lived in Moscow, succeeded in producing a
stable image on a silver plate covered with a thin
layer of gold. He soon discovered a method of
producing daguerreotypes on copper and brass
plates, which he described in *Moscow News
(Moskovskiye Vedomosti)* in May 1840. Grekov
was the first person in Russia to manufacture
daguerreotype equipment and accessories, but
at the same time he was investigating methods
of producing an image on paper, as Talbot had
done.
Grekov was also the first Russian photographer
to open an 'art studio' for anyone who wanted a
portrait 'the size of a snuffbox.' Photography
was developing along lines very similar to
painting at the time—the extremely popular
miniatures on boxes and pendants of all shapes
and sizes were no longer the province only of
painters, but of photographers as well. Unfortunately none of Grekov's portrait photographs
have survived.

'Light Painting'

We do, however, have a very well-known group
portrait by the grand old man of Russian photography, Sergei Lvovich Levitsky (1819–1898),
who also embarked on his creative career in the
1840s. The picture was taken in Rome, and
shows eighteen Russian artists and writers, including *Gogol. Levitsky knew Daguerre and
other pioneer photographers personally, and
introduced the term 'light painting' to Russia,
which made him the regular butt of ironic remarks by his literary friends.
His working life spanned fifty years, and he was
involved in the development of photography
not only in Russia, but throughout Europe, as
can be seen from the large numbers of pictures
he produced using the Daguerre method and

later the collodion and gelatine processes. In 1849 Levitsky won a gold medal at the Paris exhibition, the first time such an award had been given for a photograph. He was also the first foreigner to be given the title of court photographer to Emperor Napoleon III. Levitsky is held to have been the best of the Russian portrait photographers. He photographed four generations of the Romanov dynasty, and took part in numerous international and Russian exhibitions, sometimes serving on the jury. In fact, Levitsky was preeminent *the* expert.

He was also distinguished in the technical sphere. He made a bellows camera, and it was he who introduced optical retouching and decorative backgrounds to Russia, and also electric lighting.

Another important figure in Russian photography in the 1850s was A I Denier (1820–1892), a professional painter who did a great deal for the development of photography as an art. In 1850, undeterred by competition from numerous foreigners who were setting up studios and 'daguerreotype institutes' in the northern capital, he opened his own photographic studio in the Passage in St Petersburg.

Denier became famous for his pictures of people in high places and portraits of famous Russian writers, actors and artists. He impressed his contemporaries by the sharpness of his line, combined with a certain softness of presentation, a quality known as the 'Denier effect', achieved by printing from two different negatives.

Photographic Journals in the Early Days

With certain exceptions, extraordinarily little is known about the first decade of Russian photography and the photographers' activities. In this context the journal *Svetopis* is most interesting. It was published in St Petersburg by Auger, an artist. It ranked photography with painting and drawing as a creative skill, and was thus farsighted enough to see (as if responding in advance to much subsequent discussion) that "photography can be a science, a craft, or an art, according to the talent of those who do the work, and the purpose for which such work is carried out." This journal gives us a detailed view of the early days of photography. Its bibliographical section published criticism of Russian photographic literature, gave information on meetings of photographic societies abroad, and provided general information on Russian photography.

In the 1860s more photographic journals began to appear: in 1863 the magazine *Photographic Illustration (Fotografitsheskaya Illustraziya)* first appeared in Tver. It was published monthly, and contained rare pictures by Russian photographers of the Winter Palace, the station, the Petershof railway, monasteries in Tver, and other views. At the same time *Economy (Promyshlennost)*, a serious manufacturing and trade periodical, started to produce a supplement called *Photo Review (Fotografitsheskoye Obosreiye)*. It is interesting that its editor, Alexander Vikientevich Fribes, who had "long cherished thoughts and yearnings about publishing a photographic journal," was compelled in his introductory article to reply to "objections that photography was not in tune with the character of the magazine." He supported his point by asserting that photography "has served as a powerful instrument in various branches of industry and has brought a whole series of firms and industrial enterprises into being."

In *Photo Review* Fribes published van Mankow's popular *Useful Applications of Photography*, translated from the French, to which he added his own notes. From this time onwards he began to chronicle Russian photography. Fribes's "long-cherished thought" was fully realized in 1864, when he started to publish *Photographer (Fotograf)*, the first Russian period-

Liberals had been looking to Western Europe for decades, and in 1848 sensed Europe's failure to bring off a revolution. Left- and right-wing liberals now discovered Russia as a center of dawning Slavism. They turned to Russian tradition, and Alexander Herzen saw the Russian village community (mir obshina) as the traditional germ cell of a new, liberated society; Mikhail Bakunin hoped that Slavism would bring about the destruction of the system as it was, a *tabula rasa* on which a new community could be built.

For other Slav peoples this Pan-Slavism meant community in a new federation, but Russians could conceive of it only as "all Slavic rivers flowing into the Russian sea" (Pushkin).

New slavophiles such as N Y Danilevsky (1822–1885) developed a doctrine of cultural types. This claimed that Germano-Romance culture had exhausted itself and would be replaced by Slavic culture in world history. Others such as R A Fadeyev (1824–1883), aspired to a unification of Slavism through Russia, which he felt was possible only if Turkey and Austria disappeared from the map of Europe.

ical entirely devoted to photography. Number Three of this magazine reported that the RUSSIAN ENTOMOLOGICAL SOCIETY in St Petersburg had set up a photographic section; initiator, A I Chapakovsky, gave free lectures on photography to large audiences. Thus the year 1864 was remarkable in many respects. It marks the beginning of the period in which each stage of the development of Russian photography is documented in detail.

The editorial department of Fribes's magazine established a photographic laboratory under the direction of the experienced Chapakovsky. Here materials and methods discussed in the magazine were tried out, and reagents were manufactured for sale to the public. There was a special section in the magazine for readers' inquiries and replies from the editors.

Photographer's principal merit was that it sought "to plug gaps in technical literature" and to lay the foundations of "an independent approach to photographic questions"; it also tried to present "a complete reflection" of contemporary photography. The periodical achieved its aims, thanks to the professional competence of Russian and foreign writers. Contributions included Simonenko's *Popular Conversations on Photography* and *Readings on Military Photography; Heliochromy*, by Claude Marie François Niepce de Saint-Victor; and Schnaus's *New Dry Process*. The French writer Blanquart Evrar and the Russian Pavlenkov wrote about the relationship between photography and art.

Early Exhibitions

Russian photographers were very successful at the Berlin exhibition of 1865, further evidence of Russia's active involvement in the worldwide development of photography. In Levitsky's copious correspondence about the exhibition we read, "We can say with pride that in my opinion the best photographs shown were those in the St Petersburg photographer Bergamasco's frames; there was always a crowd in front of his work. . . . He was awarded a major medal, which he absolutely and completely deserved." Levitsky listed the principal specialisms of the Russian photographers involved in the exhibition: portraits by Bergamasco, Denier, and Dossekin (who worked in Kharkov); stereoscopic views by Okulovsky (from Pyatigorsk); Baron von Geld (from Siberia) specialized in landscapes, Borhard (from Riga) produced charcoal prints, and Shuchardt from Moscow specialized in uranium preparations. All won medals in their fields. Levitsky's final comments are interesting: "Why do we not introduce an exhibition of this kind? . . . All the European photographers and producers would definitely send their stuff."

Levitsky's dream of an international photographic exhibition in Russia was not to be realized for two decades, later, and the effort to mount it were to be wearisome. Russian photographers continued to show their work abroad. Two years after Berlin, in 1867, Russian photographers took part in the general photographic show at the Paris World Fair. The show contained works by 430 photographers, of which only 14 were from Russia.

Georgi Nikolayevich Skamoni, the inventor of heliography and most important expert on photopolygraphy, expressed an opinion which is interesting in this context. He wrote in *Photo Review*: "Of a thousand Russian photographers, there were only fourteen who decided to send their work to the World Fair. This is regrettable. Russian photographers, and particularly the St Petersburg contingent, have achieved significant and well-deserved fame, but this is recognized less in Russia itself than abroad, especially in France."

Levitsky's words sound like a response to Skamoni. In many respects they present an accurate picture of the state of Russian photography at the time: "In Russia itself, photographic ac-

Ivan Pyotrovich Raoult: Jew in the Podolsk region. (Saltykov-Shchedrin Public Library.) Odessa, 1870–1880.

Dimitri Ivanovich Mendeleyev (1834–1907). Great Russian chemist and scholar, who made significant discoveries in the field of physical chemistry. He created a periodic system of elements in 1869, on the basis of which he predicted new chemical elements and chemical qualities. He founded the RUSSIAN CHEMICAL SOCIETY in 1868, particularly with the intention of technological exploration of Russian mineral deposits. He was not accepted by the RUSSIAN ACADEMY OF SCIENCE. Because of his conflict with culture minister I D Delyanov he had to leave the University of St Petersburg in 1890.

Nikolai Nikolayevich Ge (1831–1894). Distinguished representative and founder member of the realist "Peredvishniky" movement, and regular participant in their exhibitions. He painted biblical and historical scenes with dramatic light and shade effects, and portraits, including those of Alexander Herzen and Lev Tolstoy (1884).

Ivan Nikolayevich Kramskoy (1837–1887). Realistic painter and art theoretician. Founded the "Peredvishniky" in 1870 with the Moscow businessman and patron Tretyakov, the group was committed to critical realism, and wanted to mount traveling exhibitions so that all Russia could be involved in artistic creativity, and not just St Petersburg and Moscow, as had previously been the case. He painted a series of realistic portraits of famous contemporaries (including Tolstoy, 1873, Tretyakov,1876).

Lev Feliksovich Lagorio (1827–1905). Russian naval painter, trained at the St Petersburg Academy.

tivity has developed to an extraordinary extent, but it is hidden away in various areas of our enormous fatherland, and there is no connection between them, no possibility for practitioners to prove themselves, to pass on their successes and failures."

The RUSSIAN TECHNICAL SOCIETY

However, Fribes's magazine had forged some links between Russian photographers. After it ceased publication its role was taken over by the RUSSIAN TECHNICAL SOCIETY, founded in 1866. The TECHNICAL SOCIETY had sections for technology, building and mining, architecture, shipbuilding, navigation, and artillery and armament production, but it also had a section on chemical production and metallurgy, under which heading photography was placed. Dmitri *Mendeleyev, Andreyev, Musatov, Nikolai Kulibin, and Fribes became members of the new section, and signed this supplementary declaration: "As soon as a certain number of photographers are members, on the basis of the appendix to Section 3 it will be possible to apply for the establishment of a separate section for photography."

Such a section was not established until the year 1878, but ideas were exchanged, almost on a private basis. For twelve years the "small circle of professional photographers in St Petersburg sometimes met on certain days of the week to talk about things that concerned them, but these casual conversations were not open to people who were not close to this small circle," Vyasheslav Izmailovich Sreznevsky remembers. And the plight of provincial photographers, cut off from the capital, was even worse. In comparison with *Photographer*, the new magazine *Photographic Messenger (Fotografitshesky Vestnik)*, which appeared in 1878, reported only sporadically on Russian photography. It was really just a translation of the Berlin

Photographic Society's magazine, edited by Hermann Wilhelm Vogel. The *Messenger* certainly informed Russian photographers about achievements in European photography, but practically never touched on Russian photographic theories.

In 1877–78 a supplement, *Svetopis* was published by the magazine *Svet* (*Svet* means 'light', and *Svetopis*, 'art with light'). The editors wanted to produce a magazine that was as practical and useful as possible, and so suggested to photographers that they should "send the journal statements about what interested them." But *Svetopis*, which never acquired a broad readership, survived for only two years, even though it was highly esteemed by connoisseurs for its "valuable academic character." It had printed a translation of a *Historical Sketch of the Discovery and Development of the Art of Photography*, put together from a work by Ernuf. For the first time Russian readers were able to familiarize themselves in detail with the biographies of Niepce, Daguerre, and Talbot. *Svetopis* also tried to establish contact between professional photographers and RUSSIAN SOCIETY, to which end it not only made much of the role and importance of discoveries by important European photographers, but also gave publicity to Russian photographers and their discoveries. On the cover of the magazine it said, "In order to offer *Svet* subscribers the possibility of acquiring photographs of pictures and drawings by Russian artists . . . the editors present . . . in the first place a list of excellent photographs by Karrik. I. Photographs of drawings by Mikhail Zishi. II. Photographs of pictures (Nikolai Nikolayevich *Ge, Ivan Nikolayevich *Kramskoy). III. Landscapes (Lev Feliksovich *Lagorio and Yosif Yevtafevich Krashkovsky)".

Vladimir Andreyevich Karrik (1827–1878) was a first-class artist and one of the founders of Russian genre photography. It is interesting that publicity was given to his 'reproduction photography'—a popular phenomenon in those days. Many people felt it had independent esthetic significance, because it offered access to 'genuine', 'high' art. But, because *Svetopis* obviously felt there would not be sufficient demand, it did not advertise Karrik's nature photographs—poetic landscapes, unusual pictures of peasants—which he produced in large numbers, and which were very well received at the Paris Fair. Karrik was never to experience great demand for his work, alas: his obituary appeared in the next edition of *Svetopis*. It included the evaluation that in the case of Karrik the artist was master of the technician.

The periodical *Graphic Arts Review (Obsor Grafitsheskih Iskusstv)* sang his praises as follows: "Vladimir Andreyevich conducted a constant search for portraits and views, the branch of photography that involves least work and is at the same time the most lucrative. He had set himself the task of binding photography to a genre and creating a stock of figures and scenes from the life of the people as an aid for budding Russian artists."

The use of the term "as an aid" for artists is significant. Many devotees of photography seriously thought at this time that the "photographic album ... is a school of painting that is to be taken seriously, from which every artist can draw everything he needs. ... He is now freed of the necessity of searching for his components–sky, woods, fields. It is enough ... to open the album. ..."

The majority of those interested in photography at that time took the view that one of its principal tasks was application for "artistic purposes", for example by making works of art more readily available. This view is supported by the fact that D I Mendeleyev and a group of photographic artists and amateurs had the idea of founding a special society for this purpose, but Sreznevsky recalls that "the firmly established artists' view of photography as a hindrance to the development of art hindered the common cause, even though one of those in-

volved, Karrik, had a foot in each camp. He was still alive at the time and his activities had shown the true meaning and purpose of photography. This is a further example of the utilitarian view of the aims of photography of which Karrik was victim. He had enriched its symbolic language and extended its artistic possibilities, but society saw his real creativity simply as an 'aid' to genuine art.

The magazine *Graphic Arts Review* (1878–1882) came up with another no less utilitarian, but more 'technical', approach to photography. Its editors intended to print material "which belonged directly to the sphere of printing, to typefounding, lithography, xylography, photography, and bookbinding ... thus to everything that could be connected in some way with the 'printing business' in the broadest sense of the term."

This magazine saw photography merely as a process associated with the printing industry, and was concerned above all to educate photographers by passing on practical information, but it also provides an interesting chronicle of events in Russian photographic life. It was in these very columns that the organization of the new FIFTH SECTION OF THE RUSSIAN TECHNICAL SOCIETY was described in detail: it was at last devoted to photography.

The FIFTH SECTION

It all started with the arrival of Lev Vikintievich Varnerke, connoisseur of photography and scholar extraordinaire. He was a Pole who lived in the Russian capital when he was young, but then settled in Britain. The university's PHYSICAL SOCIETY and the RUSSIAN TECHNICAL SOCIETY accepted a report on the emulsion process that he had discovered: "With his lively speech, his readiness to pass on his knowledge and experience and give information of various novelties, he gave many amateur photograph-

Vladimir Andreyevich Karrik: Konstantin Stanislavsky. 1890–1900.

Ivan Vasilyevich Boldyrev: Members of the Russian Photographic Society. (Saltykov-Shchedrin Public Library.) St Petersburg, 1878.

CRIMEAN WAR (1853–1856) The Crimean War between Russia and Turkey (supported from 1854 by a European coalition of England, France, and Sardinia) started because of Russia's provocative attitude towards Turkey, combined with an underestimation of her power. Essentially it was about "free trade": the number of English ships passing through the Black Sea had risen from 250 in 1842 to 1,741 in 1852. Nicholas I used a quarrel about the holy places of Christendom to present Turkey with an ultimatum that would have threatened Turkish autonomy had it been implemented. Russia's Pan-Slavic dreams of possession of the Dardanelles and hegemony in the Orient drove the Tsar to this hopeless move. The Western powers landed in the Crimea and conquered Sebastapol after a siege of eleven months. Russia's military and political weakness showed in its inability to relieve the town during the long siege.
As a result of this defeat a series of internal reforms were carried out, but Russia also had to come to terms with a large number of nationalist and religious ideologies.

ers the idea of coming closer together," Sreznevsky recalled.

On 22 February 1878 a farewell dinner was given in the Maly Jaroslavez Hotel in honor of Varnerke. On this occasion the photographers of St Petersburg decided unanimously to join together and organize the "Photographic Society" they had so long wished for. Sreznevsky took an appeal with twenty-three signatures to the council of the TECHNICAL SOCIETY. On 10 March a meeting took place confirming the organization of a separate FIFTH SECTION FOR PHOTOGRAPHY AND ITS APPLICATION and approved the program set up by Sreznevsky. Its aim was "the development and perfection of the technical, scientific, and artistic aspects of photography."

The section's tasks included:
• bringing together scientists and photographers,
• arranging discussions on independent research and the work of Russian and foreign photographers with critical evaluation, carrying out experiments,
• arranging exhibitions of photographic work, apparatus, and materials,
• arranging public lectures,
• printing minutes of the meeting of the Fifth Section in the society's periodical,
• exhibiting the best work of the members,
• establishing a specialist photographic library,
• and finally, setting up a photographic museum.

The chairman of the FIFTH SECTION OF THE RUSSIAN TECHNICAL SOCIETY was Dmitri Gavrilovich Birkin, who had a thorough knowledge of photographic theory and practice. The photographic section of the RUSSIAN TECHNICAL SOCIETY (which had helped by providing a photographic laboratory) began to develop the program outlined above. At one of the early meetings a lens developed by I V Boldyrev was discussed. Boldyrev was a highly talented, self-taught individual from the Don region. After his arrival in St Petersburg he registered for lectures at the Academy of Arts. His principal interest was further development and invention of technical apparatus. He perfected a lens that made it possible to take deep-focus photographs—fascinating pictures of the villages of his homeland and the Crimea. In Denier's summerhouse an experiment was carried out in which all the members of the FIFTH SECTION present were placed at random. "Despite these difficult conditions a completely sharp picture of the entire group was taken in twenty-five seconds, with perspective fully maintained," according to a report in the periodical *Graphic Arts Review.*

Svetopis took a rather different view of Boldyrev's experiment: "It seems that the lens used by Boldyrev was the usual 2 inch Germagis portrait lens.... Karelin deserves credit for the discovery of the process which Boldyrev came across independently and apparently quite by chance. The secretary of the Section, Sreznevsky, achieved results entirely independently of Boldyrev, and by a completely different route. This process was used by Laptev for his photograph ... of the principal staff studio using a three-and-a-half-inch Germagis lens. Here the various planes are even more markedly separated than in Boldyrev's attempt."

Boldyrev often provoked minor disagreements of this kind. It seems that his relationship with the FIFTH SECTION was somewhat complicated. These articles also show the level of specialized discussion of technical developments. It is also clear that Russian photographers were well aware of achievements in European photography.

Boldyrev was not to be put off by failure, however. He was very successful in constructing a shutter that made it possible to take more expressive, livelier photographs. Boldyrev also expended a lot of energy on the invention of an elastic 'asphaltlike' negative film. This could have had a considerable future if Boldyrev had been able to work under more favorable conditions, with support from the Technical Society. His invention might have been even more successful than the 'Kodak' film that George Eastman was beginning to produce in America at the same time. It would at least have provided healthy competition.

In fact the FIFTH SECTION, pillar of the Russian photographic establishment, did not offer Boldyrev even the most elementary support. This was made clear in an appraisal of his work in *Photographer.* An indignant Sreznevsky wrote in a review of a Moscow exhibition of art and industry that "for some reason or other he called himself an amateur: this led to a great deal of protest. An amateur works alone, as he wishes and ... does not use photography as a means of making a living. In a small frame all the outstanding work of his practice extending over years is exhibited.... At the bottom is the two-inch lens invented by Boldyrev.... Next to it are a few small glass items and other accessories, I do not know whether any expert attention has been paid to them, and the negative film invented by Boldyrev. This no doubt deserves attention, and could be most useful. On the table by the frame an advertisement for the exhibitor's inventions cut out of a newspaper has been fastened".

This patronizing tone contrasts strikingly with the enthusiastic praise lavished upon court photographer Charles Bergamasco's work: "Large black carved frames with mirrors sur-

FREEING THE SERFS
In 1856 Alexander II (1855–1881) said before the nobility of Moscow that it would be better to abolish serfdom from above than to wait for it to begin to demolish itself from below. This was certainly a driving force, alongside the increasing feelings of shame among intellectuals and the bourgeoisie faced with enlightened, progressive Europe. Industrialists hoped for improvements because of the potential workforce that would be released. Public opinion was dominated by discussion about freeing the serfs for years, and strongly conflicting interests argued about conditions of release. Landowners in the fertile black-earth region supported freedom without compensation, with themselves retaining ownership of the land, whereas landowners in the north—whose land was worthless but whose serfs, as people with a trade, were valuable—favored a high level of state compensation, and were perfectly happy to hand over land to the serfs. The imperial manifesto of 19 February 1861 on freeing the serfs was an all-embracing piece of legislation intended to regulate the process. Legislation intended for only specific parts of the country alone covered five hundred pages, and a map with vegetation zones and soil qualities showed various land distribution norms in 32 different colors.
There is no doubt that the liberation of the serfs was a break with the past: now everyone was guaranteed personal freedom in the sense of individual legal status but this was in no way the same as freedom of the citizen. The peasants remained bound to the legal institution of the village community (mir obshina). The community carried overall responsibility for individual taxation, which meant it was in its interest to

let no one go away. The father of a family—whose land share depended on the number of taxable, i.e male, members of his family—was concerned that his sons should stay at home. This meant that freedom of movement was restricted even after the serfs had been freed. Practice depended very much on the intellectual attitide of those carrying out the process. The purchase price, advanced by the state, had to be paid back in forty-nine years.

Ivan Vasilyevich Boldyrev: Art historian Vladimir V Stasov in a circle of painters. 1886.

round a background of soft satin in a dark raspberry color, and on this are the splendid portraits framed in noble velvet the color of dark pomegranates in fine gold bronze." Of course Boldyrev's little lenses and newspaper cuttings would find it difficult to compete with satin and bronze. What is striking is the lack of interest shown by Sreznevsky, who was secretary to the FIFTH SECTION, in the products of Boldyrev's expertise, and his complete lack of concern for the man's inventions and personality.

The 'Pan-Russian Exhibition'

In 1882 the 'Pan-Russian Exhibition' opened its doors. This was the first Russian show with a special place for photography. Here literally everything was shown that "concerned the dis-

semination of education and knowledge, the printing industry, musical instruments ... educational books ... lithography, chromolithography, typography, and finally photography, which represent a direct connection with printing."

When asked whether photography had been allocated a due amount of space at the exhibition, the reviewer for the periodical *Photography*, Sreznevsky, made a very critical appraisal of the state of photographic art, which "has not penetrated deeply enough into the soul and feelings of the Russian photographer to cause him to show ... at the exhibition studies, pictures, and portraits of which every one is lightened by thought, seized by feeling and tastefully designed. ... Nobody would have hesitated to give photography of this kind a higher place than that which it took up alongside the works of the press." At the same time the author concluded: "Many processes brought about by successes of recent times and demands that photography should be part of the world of printing make photography so closely connected with the press that it is difficult to determine the frontiers of photography in the true sense." Despite all this, it was generally felt that the presence of a photographic section at the 'Pan-Russian Exhibition' was a significant step.

Sreznevsky noted the arrival of a new figure, G S Solovev, "on the scene of photographic competition" and that he was "no commonplace photographer. All his pictures are nature studies, full of life, truth, and taste there are no artificial studio lighting effects, just natural light with no attempt to prettify it." By winning the gold medal, Solovev, in Sreznevsky's opinion "has introduced himself as a pupil worthy of his teacher Karelin's paintbrush."

This same Andrei Osipovich Karelin (1837–1906) became famous throughout Russia by winning a gold medal at the International Photo Exhibition in Edinburgh. He surprised his contemporaries most of all with his interior group

portraits. These were outstanding because of their masterly handling of spacious perspective, the play of contrasts in light and shade, and the softness of their line. At the 'Pan-Russian Exhibition' in 1882 one of Karelin's photographs, a life-size portrait of Mendeleyev, won an award. Contemporaries were impressed by the remarkable way in which it caught the scholar's nature and by its interesting technical features. Genre photographs showing the interior of a Russian peasant's house also attracted attention.

Sreznevsky also singled out the unpopular Boldyrev from the mass of exhibitors: he had won a bronze medal "for photographs taken with special methods and tricks invented by the exhibitor", no mean recognition of this quirky photographer's merits.

The RUSSIAN TECHNICAL SOCIETY's congress held as part of the 'Pan-Russian Exhibition' in Moscow was to an extent a response to the desire for a common forum. Its sessions took place in the evenings, in the MOSCOW CONSERVATORY. The text of the invitation laid great emphasis on its importance as the First Congress of Russian Photographers. Twenty-five members of the FIFTH SECTION took part, and heard four lectures by Sreznevsky and one by Levitsky. Both men were attempting to accumulate precise statistical information about photographic institutions in Russia. It was suggested that Russian photographers should be preferred to their colleagues from abroad. Another important point was that laws on photographers' copyright should be examined and brought up to date. There was also discussion about the possibility of setting up a special school of photography, a question that was to reappear at all subsequent photographic congresses.

There is no doubt that the 1882 exhibition and congress were a stimulus to the creative work of Russian photographers. Further evidence of this is given by reports on sessions of the FIFTH SECTION published in *Photographer*. These

dealt with a broad range of questions, such as Levitsky's success at the Electricity Exhibition in Vienna. The Russian expert had shown that portraits taken in artificial light were far superior to those taken in daylight in their general effect and softness of features. This dismissed a report from the Munich exhibition stating that electric light was of no use in portrait photography.

Anonymous: Peasant from Ryazan, a delegate to the State Duma. (Central Archive for Film and Photographic Documentary.) St Petersburg, c. 1890.

Fyodor Antonovich Bruni (1799–1875). He was of Italian origin, and became the most distinguished representative of academic-neoclassical Russian painting. Frescos by him and others in St Isaac's Cathedral in St Petersburg and the Church of the Redeemer in Moscow.

Lev Nikolayevich Tolstoy (1828–1910). One of the great writers of world literature. Russian and French spiritual life in the eighteenth century were of fundamental importance to Tolstoy, and the thinking of Rousseau in particular. He traveled in Western Europe then withdrew, embittered by Western materialism, to his family estate in Yasnaya Polyana. He did not associate with any contemporary groups, movements or tendencies. His novel *War and Peace* appeared between 1864 and 1869.

Grigori Yefimovich Grum-Grshimailo (1860–1936). One of the great explorers of mid and central Asia, geographer and zoologist.

Ivan Konstantinovich Ayvazovsky (1817–1900). From 1883 he studied under Maxim N Vorobiev at the St Petersburg ACADEMY OF ART, and later worked independently in the Crimea. Traveled to extend his artistic training and exhibit his paintings in Italy, Paris, Amsterdam, London, Germany, Spain, Greece, Turkey. He became the most important naval and marine painter of his time. On his return to Russia he was showered with honors. In 1847 Tsar Nikolai I made him staff painter to the Admirality. During the Crimean War he was in the siege-bound city of Sebastopol. He is said to have painted over 6,000 pictures, mainly on marine themes.

Solovev, the bright new star in the photographic firmament, was once more successful. He won a gold medal at the International Exhibition in Brussels, and a silver medal in Amsterdam. A pleasing feature is that this was seen not merely as recognition of the high esteem in which Russian photography was held in Europe, but also as confirmation of its 'artistic tendency'.

Exhibitions Everywhere

Varnerke worked tirelessly onward. He spoke enthusiastically at a meeting of the FIFTH SECTION about a series of photographs by Yevgeni Petrovich Vishnyakov (1841–1916). Vishnyakov, a full member of the RUSSIAN PHOTOGRAPHIC SOCIETY, was an explorer who had taken photographs in many regions of Russia. "His winter landscapes are particularly beautiful... despite the intense cold in which they were taken," said a report on this session of the FIFTH SECTION. Vishnyakov was one of the first professional landscape photographers. He published a book called *Travel Photographs*, and albums entitled 'Nature Photos', 'Sources of the Volga', 'Beloveshkaia Pustcha' and 'Peterhof'. These contained photographic studies and snapshots of nature alongside complicated photographic compositions.

Reports of the sessions of the FIFTH SECTION first appeared in the magazine *Photographic Messenger*, edited by P M Olchin, in 1887. A remarkable feature of this magazine was its thorough coverage of the currents of Russian photography. One of the most interesting sections was a report on the first purely photographic exhibition in Russia, held in St Petersburg in the MUSEUM OF APPLIED SCIENCE in February 1888. Its aim was to "exchange information about the state of development in various fields and areas of application for photography."

The exhibition committee was headed by en-thusiasts such as Levitsky, Varnerke and Sreznevsky. J F *Bruni, a member of the ACADEMY OF ARTS, was invited to assess the 'artistic value' of the photographs. A new and important feature was that visitors to the exhibition also had a chance of expressing their opinions. They were requested to fill in a form "with the names of two photographers who in their opinion deserved recognition."

There were 138 participants in the exhibition—firms and institutions, as well as individual photographers—and 820 photographic exhibits are listed in the catalog. Abamelek-Lasarev showed group photographs and portraits taken at the Lev *Tolstoy's home in Yasnaya Polyana, and interiors by Boldyrev taken by the light of a kerosene lamp. Subjects and genres to be evaluated by the jury included landscapes from Grigori Yefimovich *Grum-Grshimailo's expedition and reproductions of paintings by Ivan Konstantinovich *Ayvazovsky, explorations of the White Sea and Lake Onega by two engineers, Sidsiarsky and Witte, and a photographic chronicle of the life of the Tsar's family by Konrad Brandel, photographs of the eclipse of the sun in 1887, and microphotographs of a cat's spinal cord.

Awards were given to the following categories:
- application of photography for scientific purposes;
- artistic elements in the photograph;
- application of photography to printing;
- snapshots;
- improvements to photographic technology;
- portrait photography;
- enlargement of photographs.

Thus this amateur exhibition was judged by genuine professional standards. "It showed quite clearly: the expression 'amateur photographer' set against that of professional photographer in the usual sense—in other words, someone who takes portraits and considers amateurs to be dilettantes—is nowadays often not quite correct."

Anonymous: Lesson in a printing school (Saltykov-Shchedrin Public Library.) 1890–1900.

OTHER REFORMS UNDER ALEXANDER II

Pressure from the nobility and the bourgeoisie to organize public life in a more rational way by means of constitutional changes increased continually, especially after the Crimean War. Alexander thus found himself compelled to take the constitutional pressure off the state at least by responding with some reform. On 1 January 1864 "zemstvos" (village self-administrations) were set up. This name was associated with an old tradition of concept-formation which had always confronted the "country" (zemlya), in the shape of the estates and society, with the state and rule (gosudarstvo). Representatives of the nobility, citydwellers, and peasants, elected for three years in each case, were to meet as a zemstvo assembly under the chairmanship of a marshal drawn from the nobility, in order to form a zemstvo administration. This was responsible among other things for maintaining roads and bridges, upkeep of transport and postal services and of health and welfare institutions, and the extension of the elementary school system in district and province. A graded franchise assured leadership for the nobility. Zemstvos were set up originally in 33 regions, but never throughout the empire. After the attempt on Alexander II's life (1866) their powers were cut down. Then they were reactivated under Alexander III (1881–1894), and reached their peak in the twentieth century. A similar institution was the town duma (1870). The dumas effectiveness showed most clearly in the last decades of the century, when towns grew very rapidly.

After this exhibition, photographic shows were held every year in Russia. Numerous photographers from Pensa, Orenburg, and other cities showed their work at an industrial design exhibition in the Kharkov museum in October 1888. In the autumn of the same year the FIFTH SECTION approved a plan for a 'rotating exhibition in St Petersburg in 1889.' The magazine *Photographic Messenger* published the program for a 'Pan-Russian Photographic Exhibition' in Moscow.

The latter two exhibitions were intended as competing events, but "the exhibition by the RUSSIAN TECHNICAL SOCIETY on the occasion of the fiftieth anniversary of the invention of photography by Daguerre and Talbot" was particularly impressive. Visitors said the exhibition "with its many high-quality exhibits was a unique and outstanding event in St Petersburg." The Moscow exhibition was also a remarkable event in the history of Russian photography. The sensation of the show was provided by fifty-three works by M P Dmitriev (1856–1948), a photographer from the provinces unknown in the two capitals until this occasion. The set included portraits, everyday scenes, landscapes, and wonderful views of the Volga—technically flawless photographs in large format.

Dmitriev began to work for the Moscow photographer M P Nastyukov at the age of fifteen, but his real photographic training was in Karelin's studio in Nizhni Novgorod, where he made a thorough study of composition, did research into contrasts of light and shade, and learned how

INDUSTRIALIZATION

It was not just the steam engine in the factory that served as motor and symbol of technical progress, but steam engines on wheels, and in the mid-nineteenth century it was clear that railway-building would bring a great leap forward. The Crimean War showed the strategic importance of a railway network in coping with enormous distances. A great deal of building took place in the sixties and seventies in particular: In 1855 the system consisted to all intents and purposes only of the show line between Moscow and St Petersburg (a total of 1,000 versts; 1 verst = 1.06 km). In the late 1880s there were 21,000 versts, 33,000 in 1895 and 53,000 in 1902.

Industry did not start to develop at breakneck speed until the last decade of the nineteenth century, with an annual growth rate of eight percent, the period of Russia's most rapid industrial development.

Alexander Nikolayevich Benois (1870–1960). Franco-Russian painter, set designer and art historian. Founder member of "Mir Iskusstva" (World of Art). He was an outstanding illustrator and graphic designer. He designed many sets for Moscow Arts Theater and for opera and ballet. He emigrated to the West in 1917. He designed sets and costumes, but also wrote libretti for Diaghilev's Ballets Russes.

Genrich Ippolitovich Semiradsky (1843–1902). Russian painter of Polish descent. Member of the Russian ACADEMY OF ARTS from 1873, and of the Academies in Paris, Stockholm, Berlin and Rome. His work consisted mainly of effective pictures of life in ancient times. He was largely disassociated from contemporary movements.

to handle optics. After Dmitriev had accumulated a great deal of practical and artistic experience, he opened his own studio in Nizhni Novgorod. Thus the Volga area acquired an outstanding chronicler who captured famous fairs, old monasteries and hermitages, various crafts, typical characters, peasant life, and the poorest strata of the population for future generations. Dmitriev, who lived to a great age, is one of the outstanding masters of Russian photography. Dmitriev's picture series called *Volga Collection* astouned the professional photographers at the Moscow exhibition. The FIFTH SECTION devoted a talk to it. The public was amazed at the professional character of the exhibition, a new feature: many of the photographs were marked with a price and the address of Dmitriev's studio in Nizhni Novgorod, where prints could be ordered.

In April 1889 a jubilee exhibition for Russian and foreign exhibitors was held in St Petersburg. Participants were invited by a commission of experts including painters such as Ivan Ivanovich Chishkin, Alexander Nikolayevich *Benois and Alexander Karlovich Begrov, as well as Levitsky and Vishnyakov. Critics found the historical section, containing daguerreotypes, talbotypes, and heliogravures, "extremely poor", but the unusual and highly decorative idea of a balloon tethered to the ceiling and especially equipped for aerial photography was appreciated by everyone. Below the balloon was a stand showing various pieces of equipment and aerial photographs taken from considerable heights. The exhibition included aerial photographs from the balloon by Nadar, a Frenchman well known as an outstanding photographer as well as a courageous aerial navigator. Another attractive feature was his genre pictures of the inventor Chevreuil.

Russian exhibitors enjoyed particular success, with landscapes by Vishnyakov and Ivan Grigorevich Nostits and a reproduction of Semiradsky's famous painting 'Frina'. As the painting

was very large, the photographer A Konstantinovich Yershemsky used three negatives to make the print.

A critic from the *Photographic Messenger* was annoyed to find that "our amateurs specialize too little and concern themselves almost exclusively with pictures of landscapes or even portraits. ... With the exception of microphotographs we saw nothing to demonstrate how photography can be of use to medicine or the law." At the same time he noted with satisfaction that "the manufacture of photographic equipment had made such progress in the last few years that Russian products were competing successfully with foreign ones and forcing them off the home market."

So many exhibits reached award standard that the jury was forced to provide more prizes than planned. THE RUSSIAN TECHNICAL SOCIETY awarded eight medals. Ivan Fyodorovich Barshevsky was singled out for his "perfectly focused reproduction of monuments of old Russian art and for a collection of unique fullness and range of pictures of Russian archaeology." This special recognition of Barshevsky was entirely justified, as he was one of the first Russian photographers to try to record old Russian art. His work still provides valuable documentation of Russian history.

Fourteen photographers, including Dmitriev, were highly praised "for a collection of large-scale indoor portraits and sepia views," and another seventeen were given awards by the RUSSIAN TECHNICAL SOCIETY. Some of them came from the provinces, such as Yosif Tselestinovich Shmelevsky from Poltava and M O Reym from Kamenets-Podolsk. One consequence of this was that branches of the RUSSIAN TECHNICAL SOCIETY were founded shortly afterwards in Odessa, Kiev, Kharkov, Kishiniov, Khabarovsk, Baku, Tiflis, and other towns.

The magazine *Photo Amateur* was first published in 1890. Its editor and publisher, Adrian Mikhailovich Lavrov, intended it to promote

Dmitri Ivanovich Yermakov: Oil wells in Baku on the Caspian Sea. (Historical Museum, Moscow.) C. 1890.

REFORM OF RUSSIAN JUSTICE
(law passed on 20 November
1864)
The reform of justice was the
most determined act of ad-
justment to the standards of
progressive Europe. Russia
made a complete break with
its former legal system,
which dated from the time of
Catherine the Great. An
overcomplicated procedure
organized by estates, de-
pendent on the bureaucracy
and subject to all kinds of
corruption in the sense of
"class justice" for the nobility, was replaced by a simplified system following the
principles of the rule of law
and public trial.

LEGAL REGULATION OF THE
PRESS AND PUBLISHERS, 1865
Essentially all this achieved
was legalization of the practice of censorship. Thus the
government had adequate
administrative means to for-
bid things distasteful to it
without recourse to normal
legal procedures.

ARMY REFORM
In 1874 general military service was introduced to replace
compulsory recruitment
(twenty-five years, until 1859,
fifteen years). The period of
service was fixed at six years,
and could be shortened by
evidence of school education:
those who had been through
primary school had to serve
for four years, academic graduates only three months.
This was on the one hand a
great spur to becoming edu-
cated, on the other it was a
clear expression of the true
way power was distributed.

higher artistic standards in Russian photography. To this end he published information
on Russian inventions and reports on developments in photographic societies and on exhibitions and meetings. "So many wonderful
Russian inventions and applications of photography are unknown to the public, and amateurs
buy foreign stuff of no significance and no particular use simply on the basis of advertising,"
he remarked bitterly in his introduction to the
first issue. *Photo Amateur* also published information on various innovations in European
photography and analyses of specialist literature and periodicals from abroad.

Lavrov complained at first about the magazine's cool reception by the FIFTH SECTION, but
he rapidly established connections with them
and published reports of their meetings. He
also organized a 'letterbox' in the magazine for
the RUSSIAN TECHNICAL SOCIETY. Subscribers
sent in queries from all over the country, and
Photo Amateur printed answers from experts
in the FIFTH SECTION.

Lavrov also published *Amateur Photographer*
under the pseudonym A Mikhailovich, a book
on the rudiments of photography for beginners.
He also produced a *Pocketbook for Practical
Photographers and Amateurs* and handbooks
called *What Every Modern Photographer
Should Know* and *Photographer's Companion.*
He followed the copious specialized literature
with great attention. At the time this was moving in two principal directions, scientific literature for professionals and introductory literature for amateurs. Another striking feature of
the magazine was its critical style; new material
was introduced in great detail. Works reviewed
included Ilya Ivanovich Karpov's *Guide to the
Study of Practical Photography*, W I Sreznevsky's *Little Reference Book for Photographers*,
Bruno Senger's *Manual of Self-Instruction in
Photography*; Steffen's Short *Guide to Photography*, Pavel Matveyevich Dementyev's *Photographic Yearbooks*, and publications in the

Photographer's Library series by Yershemsky
and Tolkachev. Lavrov's magazine also published detailed reviews of foreign books on photography.

Changes in the Photographic Trade

Despite this, he continued to see his principal
task as the promotion of things Russian, and for
this reason published a 'Bibliography of Russian and Foreign Photographic Literature for
1885 and 1886' as a supplement to *Amateur
Photographer*, followed by *Index of Russian
Photographic Literature from 1858 to 1 January
1898*. He continued to publish this index until
1903.

Thanks to great public interest in photography
and the development of cheaper cameras, the
newspapers were full of enticing advertisements for everything new on the market in the
field of photographic technology. The modest
trade in cameras and accessories that frequently still took place in ordinary chemists' shops,
particularly in the provinces, started to increase, and was further extended in the eighteen-nineties. Photographic depots were established in St Petersburg, Moscow, and many other cities. Russian entrepreneurs were pleased
when Albert Eduard Felisch set up the first Russian gelatine-plate factory, thus placing photographic production on a more stable basis.

For this reason a report on the FIFTH SECTION's
Second Exhibition contained demands for the
encouragement of "enterprises attempting to
set up home production of those products that
are still imported from abroad." The exhibition
displayed some of these goods, including stone
sinks and developing baths, and also emulsion-
manufacturing equipment based on Adrianov's
process, a portable developing case by Kos-
satch, snapshot cameras by Freiwirt, magne-
sium flash equipment by Vasilev, and other
equipment.

Lavrov confirmed proudly: "In some processes we are ahead of foreign competition: thus for example the cassette demonstrated by Vladimirsky has nothing competing with it abroad. The lamp perfected by Kurdyunov is better than all the foreign apparatus so far introduced. Burunsky's methods for forensic photography are of a characteristic particularity so far not achieved in the West. Demchinsky's method for coating zinc plates with copper for use as printing plates is a purely Russian achievement that does not exist in foreign practice. Kozlov and Masalitinov's work on photography from a balloon shows that we are working on this question just as much as our neighbors. Suchachev's new photographic paper containing silver has the advantage over Western innovations that ... water is no longer needed to develop it, which foreign competition has not yet achieved."

It is typical that *Photo Amateur* was not satisfied merely with listing inventions, but also explained them in detail, so that amateurs could also make use of Russian products.

A Major Debate: Art and Photography

The St Petersburg exhibition of 1889 brought up the question of the principles by which works of photographic art should be judged. As usual a large number of prizes were awarded, but esthetic criteria for the judgement of photography remained as unclear as they had been twenty years earlier, and were still directed largely at achieving an approximation to "high art." The *Photographic Messenger* reviewer confirmed that "a work may not be designated outstanding if it is only good in its technical aspects, that is to say correctly developed and satisfactorily printed. Photography can only be considered outstanding if it has a considerable degree of artistic content, which depends on the ability to think the subject through and then

to light it, create an image, and retouch the photograph in such a way that is appropriate to the object represented."

These requirements were published in the Russian photographic press. They were absolutely revolutionary for their period and by no means common property throughout the world. Certainly Russian photographers were not particularly clear about 'artistic content', as is clear from an article with the significant title *What Does Artistic Content Mean in the Context of Photography?* "Is the principal role played by sharpness of image, the way the people are grouped or lighting effects?" its author asked, finally coming to the conclusion that "orthochromatism and sharpness of reproduction ... are now in the realm of scientific photography, where the services of photography are required to capture a natural phenomenon, but in modern artistic photography this sharpness is a flaw in the work."

Andrei Andreyevich Karelin, photographer son of the famous master from Nishegorodsk, made a direct appeal to make a model of the French Impressionists' blurred outlines. In this context he pointed out the possibility of making prints from sections of two or more negatives by placing them in layers.

However, sober voices also expressed the justifiable view that it was incorrect to compare photography and painting directly, but that "every art has its own framework: painting cannot offer what sculpture, architecture, music, and poetry have achieved. But to place art in some sort of order of merit, one lower and the other higher, or even to consider it a craft, is impossible.... If it is absolutely essential to establish the rank which photography should be given, then another factor of which one should not lose sight is its age."

In his assessment of results at many European exhibitions, Lavrov reached the final conclusion that it was increasingly difficult for jury members to determine the degree of artistic

NARODNIKI (Friends of the People)
"Go to the people, go among the people (v narod), there is your place, you refugees from knowledge, show ... that you are fighters, ... fighters from the Russian people!" This was an appeal from Alexander Herzen in his *Bell (Kolokol)* in 1861 to students who had been driven from the universities on the orders of the reactionary Minister for the People's Enlightenment Putyatin. Mikhail Bakunin also said "Go among the people" in 1869.
The roots of this longing for the people were to be found in the importance ascribed to the Russian village community. This was supposed to produce the new society. In summer 1873, the "crazy summer", there was a mass uprising of young students in the country among others, without any concrete reason. In the 1870s, 770 narodniki were put on trial. As with the anarchists, these young students were predominantly opposed to the state. For them the state was the personification of all evil. Narodniki saw themselves as an intellectual elite and wanted to determine the course of history. If for Bakunin it was the mass of the people itself that made history, L P Lavrov (1823–1900), his theoretical counterpole, was of the opinion that the intellectual elite would have to take over this task. Lavrov believed that painstaking work to enlighten the people would bring about the change. This dispute was known as the quarrel between the "rebels" (buntari), Bakunin's supporters, and the "preparers" (podgotoviteli), Lavrov's supporters, and was pursued particularly in emigrant magazines.

TRADES UNIONS AND STRIKES
Progressive industrialization had created conditions in the cities in the 1860s and 1870s that could—and the government saw this very clearly—lead to revolts by the workers at any time. In 1874 trade unions were banned, but there were illegal workers' organizations everywhere. In the 1880s strikes became frequent and long. It was not until 1897 though that the working day was restricted to a maximum of eleven and a half hours.

Calculations of the number of workers in the late nineteenth century vary considerably, falling anywhere between two and three million. When expressed in such figures, industrialization always seemed manageable: three million workers disappeared among a hundred million peasants.

POLICIES OF ANTISEMITIC RESTRICTION AND PERSECUTION
In 1881/2 there were pogroms leading to plunder and murder in Kiev, Odessa and other towns. The were mostly instituted by the state. In 1889 Jews were excluded from the legal profession. In 1890 they were forbidden to serve, and in in zemstvos 1892 in town dumas. In 1892 Jews were forbidden to have Christian first names. 1905 there were renewed pogroms in Odessa, a "counter-terror" tolerated by the government.

content in photographs, since "the result of the improvements in cameras and the simplification of photographic techniques is that the art of photography has been made so simple that one can even work automatically and achieve good results." He recommended that "one should be very careful in pursuing the artistic side of photography exclusively at an exhibition, and that attention should be paid to people with less talent who still produce work of significant use to science."

"What is photography? Is it art or merely mastery? These are the questions being dealt with by the English and the German press in the columns of their photographic magazines," *Photo Amateur* reported. The periodical pointed out that "the foreign press makes a distinction: it considers professionals to be masters, and amateurs to be *auteurs*."

Lavrov's magazine also pointed out this distinction, maintaining a strict division and laying particular emphasis on photographic exhibitions and competitions. Thanks to the periodical's efforts the Moscow exhibition run by the ORGANIZATION FOR THE DISTRIBUTION OF TECHNICAL KNOWLEDGE in 1892 had two separate photographic competitions—one for professionals and one for amateurs. This wide-ranging exhibition had 102 participants. Amateur work predominated, but reviewers paid particular attention to remarkable work by professional photographers who had sent in pictures of people and landscapes from the Caucasus and Siberia, and from southern and central Russia. Dmitriev won a gold medal in the professional section for "excellent nature pictures."

In Paris, where the first 'International Exhibition of Photography' took place—also divided into amateur and professional categories—Dmitriev won another gold medal. One of Russia's most famous amateur photographers, Count Nostits, produced an interesting but extremely negative view of Dmitriev's work: "I am amazed that he sent a photograph to France showing

prisoners on a building site.... The next thing will be that he shows a few banished people on their way to Siberia. But now unfortunately the dominant idea in Russia is the realist school in the manner of Monsieur Courbet of blessed memory. It is a pity that the radical Courbet could not see Dmitriev's pictures: his prisoners would have suited this fine painter's taste perfectly." Assessments of this tenor are typical both in the traditional way in which photography is compared with painting and also as a reaction of a contemporary and fellow photographer to photos in which Dmitriev had made his first attempts to document a fact, to capture real life as a chronicler might.

Russian amateurs also won awards at the Paris exhibition. Shuravlev from St Petersburg was awarded a silver medal, and Bakhrushin from Moscow a bronze.

Russia and Western Europe

In the eighteen-nineties international photographic exhibitions were no longer a rarity. The *Photographic Messenger* and *Amateur Photographer* regularly published invitiations to exhibitions, conditions of participation, and programs; they also printed Russian photographers' impressions of foreign shows: anything new to Russia in the technical, artistic or design fields was precisely recorded.

Thanks to experience gained at European exhibitions, Russian photographic magazines pressed for juries of experts to select exhibits, and for the presentation of diplomas as awards, rather than a multiplicity of medals. Their were descriptions of particular mounts popular with the English which enhanced the qualities of the photographs. A wonderful display by Eastman, from America, at an exhibition in London was introduced as a model presentation of photographic work. There is no doubt that all this enriched Russian photography, and provided good training and direction.

It was not just one-way traffic, however: foreign photographers took part in Russian exhibitions. Thus the exhibits in the section reserved for foreigners at the fourth exhibition of the FIFTH SECTION FOR PHOTOGRAPHY OF THE RUSSIAN TECHNICAL SOCIETY in St Petersburg were selected by the organizing committee. The best photographers were invited so that it was possible "to learn" from them "about presentation."

Visitors saw experiments by Professor Lipman of the Sorbonne in the field of color photography; observatories in Prague, Paris, and Heidelberg showed astronomical photography. Davidson, the secretary of the London club *Camera*, showed a collection of British photographs. Another attraction for visitors was an innovation which surprised everybody, "imitation photographs", reproducing paintings by famous artists in the same atmosphere and setting.

"The fact that only outstanding medal winners have been invited to the exhibition shows clearly how strong we are: we can be seen to be comparable with them in the eyes of the public," wrote *Photo Amateur*. An article with the characteristic headline *What Do Our Professional Photographers Lack in Comparison with Their Foreign Colleagues?* undertook a serious comparative analysis of Russian and Western European work in a *Series of letters from the Exhibition*.

In St Petersburg the work of European masters was shown *hors concours*; however, at an exhibition arranged by the RUSSIAN PHOTOGRAPHIC SOCIETY in 1896, foreign exhibitors were eligible for all four sections of the competition (scientific; artistic; technical application of photography; apparatus, instruments, materials, and accessories). The way in which medals for that exhibition were awarded shows how close were the links between European and

Russian photography, and how evenly skills had developed: silver medals for Ivanitsky from Kharhov and Werner from Ireland, for Fischer from Moscow and Nielsen from Copenhagen, Timiryasev from St Petersburg and the Panayout brothers from Bordeaux. Bronze medals were shared between Kotelov from Kazan and Byling from Dresden, Serbinov from Kertch and Grdlicke from Vienna, Dmitriev from Nizhni Novgorod and Gratl from Innsbruck. Innovations from abroad became common property almost at once, thanks to the large number of photographic magazines and the work of numerous photographic clubs and associations.

Photo Amateur provided information about the program and statutes of the RUSSIAN PHOTOGRAPHIC SOCIETY, and also detailed descriptions of European photographic organizations. The periodical also carried reports on photographic inventions worldwide, including

Dmitri Ivanovich Yermakov: Grape harvest. (Historical Museum, Moscow.) Tbilisi, c. 1890.

Anonymous: Ceremonial procession on the occasion of Tsar Nikolai II's coronation, in front of the Kremlin. (Saltykov-Shchedrin Public Library.) Moscow, 1896.

Röntgen's work on X-rays and the miracle achieved by the Lumière brothers, moving photography.

Photographic Copyright and Other Legal Matters

1896 was the year of the First Congress of Representatives of Russian Photography. (Although the 'First Congress for Photography' had taken place in 1882 in Moscow, the Muscovites still insisted on calling the 1896 congress the First Congress.) It was associated with an International Photographic Exhibition and a show devoted to the Russian Photographic Society, intended to give an idea of how rapidly the Moscow-based group was progressing. There were four key issues:

First was the application of artistic copyright to photography and photomechanical reproduction. In a lecture, Urusov identified the legal provisions applicable in suitable cases, but it soon became clear that the law was open to various interpretations, and this question bothered Russian photographers more than almost anything else: continuing development of photomechanical reproduction methods meant that their rights as authors of works of art were becoming increasingly curtailed.

A typical example is that of Dmitriev. In the photographic section of the 'Pan-Russian Exhibition' in Nishegorodsk he showed over a hundred views of the Volga—from Rybinsk to Astrakhan. Critics considered them the "most outstanding exhibit in the section," and Dmitriev was awarded a silver medal. Sytin's publishing company brought out an album of Dmitriev's pictures—without his permission—and the photographer responded with a lawsuit, which came to trial. Sytin's defense counsel claimed: "Photography requires no particular talent: the only artist involved is the sun." And therefore "photographic work [can] be the ob-

ject of a privilege, but it is in no way artistic property." The court found Sytin not guilty, but, as *Photo Amateur* wrote, "the majority of photographers remain on Dmitriev's side. He sacrificed both money and effort in order to demonstrate the extent to which photographic copyright is unprotected by existing articles of law."

This question remained unresolved at the Moscow Congress, and so did the second, which was concerned with the rights to negatives of someone who had commissioned a print. It was stressed, however, that no congress abroad had been able to solve this problem.

Opinions varied about the third question—the necessity for schools of photography in Russia. Some were in favor of founding an institution to train academics in photography as a special field; others favored setting up schools for photographic technicians; others felt that all technical schools should include courses in the fundamentals of photography. Finally the Congress concluded that it would be desirable to train photographic technicians in specialized schools and to teach photography in technical schools. The usefulness of evening lectures organized by photographic societies was pointed out.

The fourth question, on the support of photographers unable to work through age, illness, or accident proved unanswerable, although it was generally agreed to be a worthwhile and humane concern.

Questions from the Moscow forum remained topical, and continued to occupy photographic amateurs and professionals long after it closed. Thus the assembly of the RUSSIAN PHOTOGRAPHIC SOCIETY empowered A A Karelin, 'honorary member' of the ACADEMY OF ARTS, to apply for legal introduction of copyright for photographers in 1897. At that time a special commission of the ACADEMY OF ARTS involving the FIFTH SECTION and the RUSSIAN PHOTOGRAPHIC SOCIETY was also addressing the question. Most members of the commission felt that photographers

REVOLUTIONARY CURRENTS IN RUSSIA
S G Neshayev (1847–1882) wrote the "Revolutionary's catechism" with Bakunin. It begins with the following sentences: "A revolutionary is a human being dedicated to death. He has neither personal interests nor business, no personal feelings or conditions, nothing he could call his own, not even a name. Everything in him is dominated by a single passion: the Revolution." The one and only goal is destruction, "remorseless destruction". The revolutionary organization called Country and Freedom (Zemlya i Volya) came into being in 1876. At the time its working principle was still Lavrov's work on popular consciousness, but mass trials before special courts instituted by the government in 1877/8 created martyrs who accused the regime in their final speeches. The public reacted with a surprising degree of agreement to these accusations, so that the revolutionaries felt that only tsarist autocracy stood in the way of a successful revolution. In autumn 1879 Zemlya i Volya decided with a majority for planned terror. On 1 March 1881 Alexander II was killed in a second assassination attempt. This did not destroy the system, but sealed the end of the terrorist narodniki; in 1887 a small remaining circle made a vain attempt to kill Alexander III as well. Lenin's brother Alexander Ulyanov was involved in this, and was executed.

Konstantin Andreyevich Somov (1869–1939). Painter
and graphic artist, who also
studied under Ilya Repin.
Leading member of the "Mir
Iskusstva" group, and painted
mainly Impressionist.

should have the same copyright as painters, musicians, or sculptors.

However, when a law was drafted, the government again cut photographers' rights to a minimum by limiting them to five years after the work was created. One article of the law laid down that the photographer's firm and the date of the photograph should be on every print. The PHOTOGRAPHIC SOCIETY did not agree with this decision and the question remained unresolved for a many years.

The ST PETERSBURG PHOTOGRAPHIC SOCIETY

An important event for Russian photographers was the creation of the Petersburg PHOTOGRAPHIC SOCIETY in December 1897. Unlike the FIFTH SECTION, it was quite democratic in its organization, and directed not so much at stating a theory of photography as concerning itself with matters of practice. Its first events were slide competitions and photographic excursions to Olonets. At the same time photographic societies came into being in Ashabad and Semipaltinsk, in Samara and Tashkent, and also in Perm and Yelisavetgrad (Kirovgrad). They all published their statutes and programs in *Photo Amateur*, and provided regular reports on events, competitions, and exhibitions.

A SOCIETY OF AMATEUR PHOTOGRAPHERS was organized in Kiev: it took the name of DAGUERRE, and interested itself mainly in photography as an art. In Moscow a society came into being with the aim of "bringing together people concerned with photography as an art in its own right and the working out of the fundamentals of photography as an art and their dissemination." This society, under the chairmanship of Bakhrushin, a well-known local amateur photographer, staged international exhibitions in 1902 and 1903.

At the turn of the century many photographers still clung to the basic tenets of nineteenth century-painting, and this led to great confusion when they attempted to decide what was and was not artistic. An exhibition called World of Art, in which work—soon dubbed "newfangled daubs"—by Alexander Nikolayevich Benois, Konstantin Andreyevich *Somov, and Lev Samuilovich Bakst was shown, made it clear that an extremely subjective direction was being taken in the sphere of fine art. Artists abandoned their commitment to reality and sought to reproduce their own impressions by using formal painting techniques—harmony of color, rhythm of line and, interrelationships of light and shade. Photography did not have these techniques at its disposal, and consequently could not perform in the manner of "high art", nor imitate "noble painting".

For many this meant that their work had been in vain, that they had lost direction. The development of painting, the appearance of various tendencies that negated existing forms in one way or another, took a whole photographic movement into a cul-de-sac and compelled photographers to redefine their own aims. It was again necessary to rethink the difficult concept "artistic", increasingly hard to pin down because of the success of new directions in European and Russian fine art in the early twentieth century.

Critics analyzing the ST PETERSBURG PHOTOGRAPHIC SOCIETY's International Photographic Exhibition in 1903 pointed out that it not only offered "a general picture of what modern photography has achieved in matters of art and technique, but also raises the interesting question of the approach to photography in different countries." The reviewer mentioned the mass of "splendid applications of photography in science" and appreciated the extensive section demonstrating "the extent to which photomechanical printing has been perfected, based on the photographic plate," using work by members of the photo clubs of Vienna and Paris to explain to his readers how "artistry" is achieved by composition, lighting, and printing on matt paper, and also by using attractive mounts. European and Russian photographers alike were keen to find untraditional and experimental solutions, but photographers continued to try to keep up with modern painting, particularly in following some of its odder trends.

The magazine *Svetopis*, which reappeared starting in 1907, stated its aim quite openly in its inaugural article warning "against enthusiasm for fashionable, occasionally ugly, trends." An article by Produkin-Gorsky in *Photo Amateur* is shot through with concern about the search for form: "I came across a piece of advice from a 'photographic impressionist', who writes that to achieve an effect one should loosen the lenses a little. . . . Possibly one would wish to show individual understanding of the subject, not reproduce nature as it is, but rather as it seems. But this is untrue, as nature appears to nobody as it is depicted in many photographic supplements to magazines. However, photography is, as must be admitted, an art with a recording character."

An author in the magazine *Photographic Messenger (Vestnik Fotografii)*, the organ of the RUSSIAN PHOTOGRAPHIC SOCIETY, put forward a directly opposing point of view: "In photography as in painting the artist should reproduce nature not precisely, that is to say, two or three patches, a few strokes from the hand of the artist, can give incomparably more than a report captured on a plate by a modern lens."

Photography as Documentation —and in Color

Numerous debates arose in Russia about problems of art and photography. But at the same time an International Congress of Documentary Photography was being held in Marseilles, and this confirmed the quality of photography as a useful document in various branches of science, art, and industry and discussed reproduction procedures for documentary photos and questions on how technical durability could be guaranteed. All this was clear evidence of the discovery of other, new possibilities in photography and fascination with possibilities for reproduction and duplication of pictures.

Not a single Russian photographic magazine reacted to this development. And when *Photo Amateur* reprinted an article called *War Photography* from a French magazine there was no response at all. This was absolutely typical, and shows how narrowly the horizons of discussion were being drawn at this stage. It must be remembered that the Russo-Japanese War was being fought, and that the Japanese combined photography and spying quite brilliantly by taking aerial photographs showing Russian troop movements. The editor did point out that people interested in information of this kind for professional reasons would draw their own conclusions from the article. (The First World War showed that this had not been the case.) But, as we have said, Russian photographers did not react at all to these new pieces of information, all sensational for their period.

At that time a whole series of photography magazines existed in St Petersburg: *Photographic Messenger (Vestnik Fotografii)*, *Practical Photographer (Fotograf-Praktik)*, *All Russia (Vsya Rossiya)*, *Light-Painting (Svetopis)*, *News of the Russian Society of Amateur Photographers (Izvestia Russkogo obstshestva Liubitelei Fotografi)* and also *Photographic Sheet (Fotografitshesky Listok)*, and *Photo News (Fotografitshesky Novosti)*. They were all principally interested in the new sensation, color photography, and its artistic advantages were thoroughly analyzed.

The most popular of these magazines was *Photo Amateur*, edited by Prokudin-Gorsky. Its

UNION FOR THE LIBERATION OF THE WORKING CLASS
The notion of a political organization of social-democratic workers was realized by Julius O Cederbaum (1873–1923) who had been writing under the pseudonym Julius Martoc since 1894, and I N Ulyanov (1870–1924), who took the name Lenin in exile in Siberia, when they founded the Union for the Liberation of the Working Class (Soyuz Borby za Osvobotshdenie Truda) in 1895, thus bringing together all the Marxist groups in St Petersburg. In December 1895 and January 1896 the Union was dissolved, even before the first number of its illegal newspaper *The Matter of the Workers (Delo rabotshego)* had appeared. Its leaders, including Martov and Lenin, were sent into exile in Siberia.

RUSSIAN SOCIAL-DEMOCRATIC WORKERS' PARTY
In March 1898 representatives of various groups in Minsk founded the Russian Social-Democratic Workers' Party (RSDRP). Lenin joined it in 1899. In *What Do We Do? (Shto delat)* Lenin addressed himself to the question of organization. At the second party congress, which opened on 30 July 1903 in Brussels, and moved to London a little later because of the police—there was a split. The majority of the congress (majority = bolshinstvo, hence Bolshevists) had its way in questions of the statute.

SOCIAL REVOLUTIONARIES
The Party of the Social Revolutionaries grew out of the unification of the 1890s narodniki groups in 1901. They, in marked contrast to the Marxists, wished to achieve peasant socialism with an

Anonymous: The first multi-seater with passengers on the Vladimirsky Prospekt, outside house number 17. St Petersburg.

ideological combination of popularism and reforms. The party supported the provisional government and opposed the Bolshevists from November 1917. The social revolutionaries used individual terror in their fight against tsarist autocracy; their "fighting organization" murdered interior ministers Sipyagin (1902) and Pleve (1904), Grand Duke Sergei Alexandrovich (1905), and prime minister Stolypin (1911). In 1917 the party increased in size because many of the intelligentsia joined it. It had about 400,000 members and provided several members of the provisional government, including Kerensky. After the unsuccessful revolt in the summer of 1918, the "social revolutionaries of the right" who had not fled or been liquidated were eliminated by the Bolsheviks between then and 1922.

articles and magnificent color supplements demonstrated the possibilities of this new development in photography: Prokudin-Gorsky saw this is as the journal's principal role.

There was no doubt at all that color photography really was art. It was no coincidence that in March 1908 color slides by Chegolev of St Petersburg occupied the leading place in in the International Exhibition of the Moscow SOCIETY FOR ART PHOTOGRAPHY. Then the high point of a four-day exhibition in May at the ACADEMY OF ARTS put on by representatives of the eleven Russian photographic societies was a screen presentation by Prokudin-Gorsky called "Photography in Natural Color", intended to show that photography is high art.

The International Photographic Exhibition in Kiev very much reflected the spirit of the times. The first section, "Art photography", included two sub-sections for color photography and slides. And at the 'Second Congress of Russian Representatives of Photography' attached to the exhibition, both Stefan Vasilyevich Kulshenko and G G de-Metz lectured on color photography. But the Congress once more gave the lion's share of its attention to the question of teaching in the various branches of photography, and to techniques of photographic reproduction. There was much fairly concrete discussion about the example of the Kiev Applied Arts Workshop for Printing. Kulshenko presented a report on its work, and also spoke about heliogravure techniques.

The Congress passed a resolution in support of the activities of the 'Kiev school' and demanded that more money be made available. At the same time it turned to the RUSSIAN PHOTOGRAPHIC SOCIETY with a suggestion from the wellknown photographer Sergey Lobovikov from Vyatka. This noted three basic conditions for the conduct of exhibitions:

1 no awards other than diplomas;
2 selection of a jury of competent persons, announcing in advance how it is made up;

3 only accepting those exhibits which are of exclusively artistic interest.

The last of these decisions was highly topical, because at the majority of the exhibitions then being organized across the country, no preselections were made by the provincial societies. For this reason the local jury, often underqualified, awarded an excessive number of gold and silver medals and other distinctions that just happened to be around, but did not necessarily have any real status. This naturally lowered standards, which was the principal cause of concern.

In the opinion of the informed public Russia made an extraordinarily feeble impression at two world exhibitions—the 1909 International Exhibition in Dresden and the 1910 show in Budapest. These were exhibitions of entirely different character. The Dresden exhibition was on a gigantic scale. Seventeen sections showed achievements in art photography from all over the world, and demonstrated the numerous applications possible in science, technology, and industry. In contrast the exhibition in Budapest was something of a chamber show, giving a picture of art photography in various countries.

Many feared serious loss of prestige for Russian photography on the world stage. The chairman of the DAGUERRE SOCIETY, Nikolai Alexandrovich Petrov, a distinguished Russian portrait photographer, writing in the *Photographic Messenger*, was quite justified in saying that much work by Russian masters does not appear at international exhibitions and in foreign newspapers because from the European point of view they are of no artistic interest.

Someone writing in *Photo Amateur* explained this as follows: "Generally speaking the problem with Russian work is not a degree of backwardness, but relative modesty of subject and technique in execution. There is a lack of striking external effects in most of the pictures. This is probably caused by the more modest nature of the Russian character and way of life, and by reasons of a technical nature, which are in their turn connected with the difficulties faced by amateurs in Russia: it is only rarely that they will have an adequate selection of material available in their own home."

On the other hand, Petrov saw the principal reason for the low standard of Russian photography in a lack of general artistic development, and felt that photography journals should play a greater role. He compared the situation in Russia with the West, and pointed out that Germany for example had over twenty photographic magazines, whereas in Russia in 1911 only three remained. The most distinguished of these was the Moscow magazine *Photographic Messenger*, the organ of the most important, richest photographic organizations in the country: the RUSSIAN PHOTOGRAPHIC SOCIETY, the ODESSA PHOTOGRAPHIC SOCIETY and a whole series of provincial photographic associations. Besides these there were two St Petersburg magazines published by well-known photographic firms, *Photographic Sheet*, published by Jochim and devoted to photographic technique, and the *Journal of Practical Photography*, published by Steffen. The Muscovites thought that the St Petersburg publications were not "free" in character, too passionless, more like price lists and catalogs, essentially commercial and intended merely to advertise their respective firms.

The St Petersburg magazines had a lavish supply of advertisements for cameras, lenses, and photographic accessories and gave thorough reports on how such materials should be used. Most of them came from abroad and were indeed in tune with the business interests of the firms financing them, but nevertheless, or perhaps precisely for this reason, their program was rather more broadly based. It was therefore generally recognized that they had "done not a little for photographic competence and the dissemination of technical knowledge in Russia." This is particularly true in the case of the *Journal of Practical Photography*, which attempted to serve the broad range of "practical workers," beginners as well as professionals. While the Moscow-based *Photographic Messenger* felt itself drawn to "photographic art," the *Journal of Practical Photography* paid a lot of attention to *Scientific Photography* as well as *Practical Photography*: articles by Russian and foreign authors on *Astronomical Photography*, *Photography from Flying Machines*, and other such subjects were printed.

The 1912 International Exhibition in St Petersburg

In April 1912 the *Journal of Practical Photography* organized an all-embracing international exhibition in the galleries of the SOCIETY FOR THE FURTHERANCE OF THE ARTS in St Petersburg. It was divided into the following sections:

1 Application of photography for scientific and forensic purposes;
2 Works by photographers and photographic societies (portraits, views, genre photographs);
3 Color photography;
4 Cinematography;
5 Photomechanical processes;
6 Photographic industry;
7 Photographic literature.

THE RUSSO-JAPANESE WAR
Russia's expansionist policies in the Far East and Japan's aspirations to great-power status led to severe tension about control of Manchuria and the Liaotung peninsula in the 1890s. This tension reached its height in early 1904, when the Japanese destroyed the Russian war fleet in Port Arthur. After a series of defeats, Russia had to make concessions to Japan at the Peace of Portsmouth of 5 September 1905. The war did not significant impair Russian power in the Far East, but did contribute to a severe political crisis at home and strengthened the revolutionary movement in Russia.

THE REVOLUTION OF 1905
A strike at the Putilov works in the early days of 1905 led to a walkout throughout St Petersburg. On 9 January there was a mass demonstration outside the Winter Palace. An elite unit attacked the workers, who were carrying pictures of the Tsar and icons, with brutal armed force. As a result of this Bloody Sunday strikes increased all over the country. Strike committees were formed everywhere and joined together in councils (soviety) of worker-delegates. The soviets developed from organs of proletarian self-administration into headquarters of the political revolutionary struggle. The peasants also created an organ to represent their interests in the Peasants' Union (Krestyansky Soyuz) and in November 1906 demanded nationalization of all land for the benefit of the people who worked on it.

Ilya Yefimovich Repin (1844–1930). One of the greatest realist painters. Member of the "Peredvishniky" group, about 1890 moved closer to the "Mir Iskusstva" group. He was at the height of his powers in the 1870s and 1880s. His work was influenced by Impressionism and Symbolism. After the October Revolution he lived on his estate, which by then was in Finnish territory.

Student from St Petersburg. 1915.

Sreznevsky, photography's oldest champion and a member of the magazine's editorial team, was chairman of the exhibition committee. Thanks to his energy and experience, over two thousand Russian and foreign exhibitors took part in the exhibition. A twenty-two-man jury selected the material. Stereoscopic pictures of medical operations were placed in a series along with pictures presented by the St Petersburg police; large-format pictures taken by an aircraft from the officers' flying school hung alongside photographs of new types of plants from the Botanical Gardens; an album of documentary photographs on plague in Manchuria was placed alongside photographs of writing equipment from the Pavlovsk Observatory. K K Bulla, of the famous St Petersburg photographic family, brought a large number of "illustrative photographs" to the exhibition, all of which had appeared in magazines and newspapers.

Photographers from Vienna and Odessa, from St Petersburg, Munich, Riga and Rome, members of numerous foreign and Russian photographic societies, showed their work at the exhibition. But the oldest and most significant society, the RUSSIAN PHOTOGRAPHIC SOCIETY, did not take part. It published an article by Petrov in its organ *Photographic Messenger*. It was called *Photographic Exhibitions and Photographic Art*, and was sternly critical of the idea of such an "all-embracing" exhibition, in which there was no special section for art photography, and works of "high photographic art" were compelled to take their place alongside prosaic objects from the photographic industry. In Petrov's opinion this was reminiscent of an exhibition in which *Repin's pictures were shown alongside the paints with which they were painted.

The editors of the *Journal of Practical Photography*, who admired Petrov's organizational abilities and experience in running international exhibitions, had sent off two invitations to Petrov simultaneously, in order to persuade him to become a co-organizer of the St Petersburg exhibition. Petrov justified his clearly worded refusal by saying that *Photographic News* was not up to the task. The photographers from St Petersburg were understandably offended, and pointed out that their program was practically identical with the one devised by the RUSSIAN PHOTOGRAPHIC SOCIETY.

These squabbles are worthy of mention because they make particularly clear the different view of the significance of photography in St Petersburg and Moscow. The Muscovites explained their refusal simply by saying that they were were defending the rights of "pure" art photography, for which independent exhibitions were needed. The photographers of St Petersburg interpreted the concept of photography much more broadly by including, for example, its numerous "applications" in science and industry.

'Light Painters' and 'Photographers'

The difference in the interest of the St Petersburg and Moscow photographers clearly shows two opposing schools of thought, on both the artistic and technical levels. *Photographic News (Fotografitsheskiye novosti)* published a wide-ranging article on the subject, *Aims and Means*. It said that, in the eyes of the ST PETERSBURG PHOTOGRAPHIC SOCIETY, professional photographers applied considerable energy to achieving technical perfection, and were thus a quite specific group. For them "photography as such was the goal," but esthetic perfection was a means of enhancing the significance of their work.

But there was another, younger generation of 'light painters' who had started to concern themselves with color photography after its teething toubles had passed; the process of producing faultless photographs had thus been considerably simplified. It was this group, whose ideas were shared by members of the Kiev DAGUERRE SOCIETY and also latterly the RUSSIAN PHOTOGRAPHIC SOCIETY with its *Photographic Messenger*, which now represented the view, contrary to earlier tendencies, that "art is the goal the photographer is striving for, and technical aspects are only the means of achieving that goal." The author, who said the 'photographers' were tending towards an academy of painting, dominated by tradition, but where technique dries up talent, and compared the 'light painters' with 'free movements,' where possibilities of individual artistic expression exist. He concluded by saying that in the interests of photography as art the most recent trend was to be welcomed in every way.

But by no means everyone shared this view. It was important that it was not always supported, even by members of the RUSSIAN PHOTOGRAPHIC SOCIETY and readers of the *Photographic Messenger*. But it was this magazine that from 1911 to 1913 became the vehicle for the ideas of the young 'light painters', years in which Petrov was in charge of the artistic department.

Petrov published work by foreign and Russian masters, presented in the same way, in the *Photographic Messenger*. This placed traditional photographs (such as photographs by the extraordinarily popular genre photographer Lobovikov, known as Wanderer to photographers) alongside work by innovators from the 'Molodoye Iskusstvo' (Young Art) group. Work by Trapani, Murzin, and Savrasov, with blurred outlines and no distinct contours, tending towards a strange symbolism, deliberately strove to look like painting or drawing in the arrangement of subjects and particular formal traits.

Work by members of 'Young Art'—Trapani, Savrasov, Levenson, Svishov, Ivanov-Terentev, and others—were still regularly printed in the *Photographic Messenger*, but fierce polemic against them continued to appear in the press. It is typical that the logic of such articles was based on postulates put forward by opponents

Anonymous: A Valceva, interpreter of gypsy ballads.

THE END OF THE REVOLUTION
In the manifesto of 1905 Ni-cholas II (1899–1917) granted his Russian subjects without difference of station the ba-sic rights of free citizens: in-violability of the person, freedom of conscience, speech, assembly, and corpo-ration. In principle he also granted universal franchise and promised to give the state duma the exclusive right to guard the legality of the adminstration.
The liberal party of "consti-tutional democrats" was the strongest group in the duma in May 1906, with 178 mem-bers. On 9 July 1906 the Tsar dissolved the duma and or-dered new elections.
P A Stolypin (1862–1911), the former minister of the inter-ior, became prime minister. Revolutionary terror in-creased. In 1906/7 there were hundreds of assassina-tion attempts and thousands of victims. There were sev-eral organized revolutionary parties. Stolypin only just es-caped a plot that led to the death of thirty-two people in his house and consequently he attempted a systematic beating back of the revolu-tion. In 1907 the revolution petered out. Stolypin secured conservative majorities in the duma by new electoral legislation. His policies, stamped with Greater Rus-sian nationalism, destroyed all the revolutionary acquisi-tions of the Russian nation-alities. His agrarian policy was a carefully attempt to in-crease productivity by devel-opment of individual strengths. Stolypin was re-sponsible for questionable policies which nonetheless at least had recognizable aims. On 1 September 1911 another attempt on his life was made in the Kiev opera house, and he died five days later.

of 'leftist' trends in painting. "Excessive zeal is setting in with this 'photographic futurism,' with these patchy pictures with shrieking titles. … It is obviously not difficult to make huge enlargements, to dissolve a clear image pro-duced by the lens into indistinct patches of white, grey and black. … It is much easier to imitate Futurist pictures than to try to produce a negative which is art in itself, in its very being, and as a consequence of this ease excessive en-thusiasm for formless photography is growing not only in the West, but here in Russia as well." As we can see, opinions continued to diverge. Some felt that the Futurists were destroying form and drawing, "taking away photography's one valuable feature," and that "photography does not need to be ashamed of its own mecha-nism, nor to put on the mask of free painting." Others asserted that "works of the old school … were too mechanical" and had limited the free-dom of the photographer.

Supporters of these two opposing views came together at the Friendly Exhibition of Work by Members of the RUSSIAN PHOTOGRAPHIC SO-CIETY, which was held without jury or awards. An unlimited number of works were accepted, which were executed "by any photographic process, including artistic, scientific and rec-ord photography." This exhibition, which was unambiguously 'conciliatory' in character, was one of the last major exhibitions, despite its re-gional nature, before the Revolution.

War

The First World War made a drastic difference to everyday life in Russia, and of course had an effect on photography as well. An international competition organized by Kodak on the entirely typical subject of Moments of Joy and Happi-ness was practically the last contact with col-leagues abroad. But the worst feature of these years was not that Russian photography was

starting to be isolated, but its complete lack of economic security, which became immediately apparent under war conditions.
The Photographic Messenger was concerned with discussion of artistic matters, and was compelled to point out "the sad fact that we re-ceive most everyday photographic supplies from Germany, England and, France" and "our photographic industry remains embry-onic for the time being." The editors published detailed and very eloquent figures on the "ex-port of photographic products from Germany and Austria," then returned to their beloved esthetic polemics. The only positive program undertaken was to point out the necessity of establishing a college for the study of photog-raphy and the mechanics of photography, and of revitalizing Russian photographic literature.
The St Petersburg Journal of Practical Photog-raphy was against the foundation of a college, saying that it was a matter for the government, but the RUSSIAN PHOTOGRAPHIC SOCIETY must carry out the resolution of the 'Second Con-gress of Photographers' and set up a network of schools to train qualified practitioners. This group, after securing the needs of the Russian photographic industry could then provide stu-dents for higher education in the subject.
Unlike the narrowly 'artistic' Photographic Messenger, the St Petersburg Journal of Practi-cal Photography published an article by Srez-nevsky called The Task Facing the Modern Pho-tographic Industry. This listed immediate objectives—establishing an optical factory in Petrograd, development of chemical produc-tion in Kiev, and the extraction of bromine and iodine from seaweed from the Black and White Seas—a series of concrete projects. The author stated with regret that he had pointed out as early as 1896 that Russian photography was 85 percent dependent on imports from abroad. But it was not until the war and the hard condi-tions it imposed came along that the govern-ment and the photographic public were com-

pelled to concern themselves with the technical requirements of photography.

Even though almost every issue of the *Journal of Practical Photography* reported measures aimed at securing the photographic industry, there was still a severe lack of essentials. The *Journal of Practical Photography*, the *Photographic Sheet* and the *Photographic Messenger* all published an appeal to their readers: "The military authorities need lenses suitable for photography from flying machines and balloons: give your lenses for aerial photography. Professional and amateur photographers, do your duty to the Motherland! Remember that victory may depend on knowledge gained from the air." In this context we should remember the article *Photography and War* dating from 1905 about the equipment of the Japanese army. At the time this article produced no response in the newspapers, and it would seem from the critical situation in 1915 that it also went unheeded by the military authorities.

Photographic reportage

While the *Photographic Messenger* was largely filled with arguments about 'gloomy' futuristic photography, the *Journal of Practical Photography* printed numerous articles on current matters, e.g., *War and Aerial Photography* and *Photography and Geophysics*. The magazine was illustrated with news photographs by K K Bulla. He recorded the most important events in the northern capital. K K Bulla was the founder of a whole dynasty of photographers and also of Russian news photography as a genre. He tended not to be taken seriously by his contemporaries because of their penchant for 'art photography'.

Bulla photographed rallies and demonstrations, Duma meetings, Tsar Nikolai II visiting maneuvers, the arrest of the Provisional Government, and the women's Death Batallion. He

produced an extremely interesting and masterly chronicle of events in St Petersburg in these historic times. In the *Journal of Practical Photography* in May 1917 an article entitled *Petrograd and Its Life as Subjects for Artistic Photography* was printed, stating that "majestic St Petersburg, similar in character to foggy London, produces many subjects for the true photographic artist." Bulla took extremely interesting portraits, both in composition and psychological charcateristics, of almost all the outstanding figures of Russian culture, a unique 'Russian Pantheon', but in the columns of the photographic magazines boring portraits by provincial amateurs were analyzed, and deep and thoughtful articles published about problems of portrait lighting and composition.

There was only a single small note, headed *Photography for the Press*, dealing with awakening interest in photographic reporting and giving technical advice on printing and enlarging pictures of this kind. A much more concrete and thorough article called *War Photography* appeared in 1915 in the *Moscow Magazine* and in the *Russian Photographic Messenger* in Odessa. Its author was J Melodiev, a representative of the RUSSIAN PHOTOGRAPHIC SOCIETY. He wrote about the difficulties of taking photographs under military marching conditions and stressed that the photographer's hand did not raise his camera "to capture all this horror. ... This is not our affair, ... for something that would be a treasure for specialists is not for us." This article showed clearly the "photographic artist's" attitude to photography by reporters and correspondents. This servant of "artistry" even sent back landscapes and pictures of women in beautiful interiors from the front.

This contemptuous attitude to 'recording' photography explains to a certain extent why the problem of photographic reporting as a genre with all its particular features and rules was not on the agenda. Here again was the much-discussed problem of the training of photograph-

FIRST WORLD WAR
The great obstacle in the way of realizing any political community of Slavs or even the southern Slavs, was the Habsburg monarchy in Austria-Hungary. Russian politics before the First World War can to some extent be explained by this fact. The question of nationalities—which had come to a head in the Balkans—and also the obligations of alliances would not permit a conflict with Austria-Hungary to be an isolated one; the result was the greater conflict of the First World War. At its end the shape of Eastern Europe was fundamentally changed, and three European empires met their end.

In 1914 St Petersburg was renamed Petrograd, and it has been called Leningrad since Lenin's death in 1924.

ers, a sore point which was not solved despite Congress resolutions up to 1917. Photography courses sprang up sporadically here and there, sponsored by this or that society, but there was practically no institution offering continuous, purposeful teaching.

Photography was taught in some institutes of higher education, however. Prokudin-Gorsky taught at the COLLEGE OF TECHNOLOGY in St Petersburg, Prileshaev worked at the COLLEGE FOR RAILWAY ENGINEERING, and Petrov was on the staff of the POLYTECHNIC in Kiev. But despite this they provided neither a serious academic training in photography nor training from the craft and technical point of view.

Phototechnical courses, conducted by L J Mikhailov-Muchkin, editor of the Odessa journal *Russian Photographic Messenger*, started with the support of the MINISTRY OF EDUCATION, but not until 1916. These courses were practically the first specialized training institution for photography in Russia. Moscow did not introduce courses of this kind until July 1918.

The *Journal of Practical Photography's* appeal to its readers is typical of this period: "The knowledge borne by us in the great family of photographers is a tiny grain of that mass of knowledge that the Russian people needs. May Russia be covered with a network of teaching institutions!" Besides this appeal in the spirit of the revolutionary period, Yermilov, the editor of the paper, printed a very full teaching program for academic and technical institutions at all levels.

In January and February 1918 the COMMISSARIAT FOR POPULAR EDUCATION approved Yermilov's project, to which it had added a resolution of its own: one of the centers should collect photographs and reproductions of masterpieces of Russian photography, in order to make further dissemination of the country's art treasures possible.

In March the STATE COMMISSION FOR POPULAR EDUCATION approved the creation of a special committee for the furtherance of photography and photographic knowledge. Here a program was worked out for a college for laboratory technicians and technical staff in the field of photography and film and for the training of mechanics for the manufacture of cameras, equipment, and shutters.

In July a council of eleven people started on the practical organization of the COLLEGE OF PHOTOGRAPHY AND PHOTOGRAPHIC TECHNIQUE. The plan was to organize faculties for scientific education, art photography, trade, industry and photomechanics as well as popular scientific course for the masses and a system of students in faculties—a new stage in the development of Russian, and now Soviet, photography.

Anonymous: On the Neva. Ice being taken away on the Tushkov quay, seen from the Stock Exchange Bridge. The ice was needed by warehouses, usually to keep food cool. It was stored for weeks under sawdust in cellars without melting. St Petersburg, 1903.

Tatyana Saburova

Reminders of Russian History

The archives of the STATE HISTORY MUSEUM, Moscow

Alexander Ivanovich Herzen (1812–1870). Philosophical and political writer, publicist, associated himself with the Hegelian Left. Arrested because of revolutionary activities and exiled to Siberia for two and three quarter years. In Moscow he and Belinsky were leaders of the radical group of Western sympathizers. He left Russia for ever in 1847. In London he founded the magazine *The Bell* (1857–67). Deeply disappointed in Western socialism, he hoped to see it realized in Russian village communities.

Ivan Sergeyevich Turgenev (1818–1883). One of the great Russian prose writers. Studied philosophy, with particular emphasis on Hegel and classical philology at the universities of Moscow, St Petersburg and Berlin. He spent most of his life abroad, from 1854 almost exclusively in Baden-Baden and Paris, but maintained close links with Russia. He rejected the "Slavophiles" and associated himself with those who sympathized with the West. His work was much influenced by his unrequited love of the singer Pauline Viardot-Garcia.

The HISTORY MUSEUM has a very full collection drawn from the first hundred years of photography. The catalog suggests that photographs were among the museum's earliest acquisitions. There was good reason for this. The museum was established on the initiative of the Sebastapol branch of a Polytechnic Exhibition opened in Moscow in 1872. The huge success that this exhibition enjoyed with the public gave its spiritual fathers the idea of founding a museum to house significant items from the history of the country. Later the Sebastapol exhibits were taken into the archive of the HISTORY MUSEUM. They included photographs from the period of the Crimean War (1853–1856).

In the course of time the photographic archive grew, particularly on the basis of gifts from the distinguished Russian collectors Bakhrushin and Chyukin, who bequeathed their collections to the HISTORY MUSEUM at the turn of the century. After the October Revolution the collection took over photographs from other museums and institutions.

In order to be able to determine the value of a photograph properly, it first has to be read, to answer a whole series of questions: Who or what event does this represent? Who took it, when and where? It is also important to establish whether the photograph is genuine—in other words, whether it is an original print or not, as valid research into our photographic inheritance is possible only using originals.

One set of photographs in this collection that is particularly interesting in historical terms covers the armed rebellion in Moscow in December 1905, and gives a remarkable insight into socio-economic conditions in prerevolutionary Russia. Another section of enormous value is the daguerreotypes. The HISTORICAL MUSEUM has 278, the most extensive collection in the Soviet Union.

Daguerreotypes technique was difficult, and meant that only a single copy could be produced. Most daguerreotypes are portraits: pleasing miniature pictures on silver or silvered-metal plates, reproducing subjects' features with "unusual truth and faithfulness to reality." Subjects include the Decembrist Volkonsky; *Herzen, the revolutionary and democrat; *Turgenev; Cherbina, a poetess; Sabelin, a historian; Garnovsky, a Moscow University professor; Polina Biardo, a singer; Chomyakov, a journalist; Ketcher, a translator and doctor; Chertkov, a rare book collector; and many other distinguished Russians. Most of the people depicted in the daguerreotypes are unidentifiable, however.

Some daguerreotypes have identifying labels, which make it easier to understand particular items. The portraits of Volkonsky, "state criminal in the case of 14 December 1825," and of his wife Maria Nikolayevna, who followed her husband "into voluntary exile," are of interest in this context. The photographer was Davignon,

Karl August Bergner: Mother of the patron Savva Ivanovich Mamontov with her daughters. Moscow, c. 1855.

who went on a business trip to Siberia in 1845. Here he took photographs for certain clients. Some of his customers were Decembrists living in a settlement just outside Irkutsk. Fate decreed, however, that the pictures fell into the hands of the authorities in the course of his journey, and were used as a corpus delicti in special proceedings against the "artist Davignon" instituted by the THIRD DEPARTMENT OF THE CHANCELLERY OF HIS IMPERIAL HIGHNESS. But the Decembrists managed to hide some of the daguerreotypes. Portraits of the Volkonsky family were among those that evaded seizure and subsequent use in the case against Davignon.

The arrested daguerreotypist had great difficulty in proving that he had not been acting with malicious intent against the government. Davignon had to make a written declaration that he had not retained "a single portrait of a political criminal taken in Siberia" and swore under threat of severe penalties that he would "not take any more pictures of the said criminals." The proceedings were dropped, but not before they had caused a great deal of unpleasantness for Davignon, finally bringing his career in Russia to an end. The only 'positive' thing to come out of it was that Davignon's name as a daguerreotypist now had a 'particular cachet'.

Martin Abadi's daguerreotypes are also outstanding. His studio, in Petrovka Street, was one of the most popular in Moscow, and his portraits were produced at a time when daguerreotypes were at the high point of their short history (1838 to about 1851). An advertisement for the 'Abadi Gallery for Daguerreotype Portraits' said in 1850: "People stop involuntarily in front of these truly living portraits and can only be amazed by an art in which the joint strengths of nature and man have brought portraiture to a peak of perfection, and precision, and above all provides a convincing likeness."

Another reason for the large number of portrait photographs in the HISTORY MUSEUM is prob-

ably that the relevant department was for a long time called the 'Department of Iconography'. Its principal task was to acquire a collection of portraits of notable personalities in Russian history. But even allowing for this bias, the collection shows the predominance of portrait photography over other genres in the early decades.

As far as esthetic value is concerned, the portraits are of differing quality, and in some cases commercial considerations were clearly dominant. The portraits show how the working style of photographers changed over the decades and creative aims were altered. This chapter takes a closer look at the creative legacy of the artists who can be considered classicists of Russian photography, particularly those whose work shows no tension between art and financial considerations.

Much has already been written in Russia about Levitsky and Denier. They played an outstanding role in the development of photographic art in Russia, both as talented portraitists and as inventors in the field of photographic technique, and won the highest awards in Russian and European exhibitions.

Levitski had some interesting commissions. They often show him to be an artist with the knack of capturing the essence of his subject's character, as is the case with portraits of Volkonsky and Herzen. Shelgunov, a revolutionary and eye-witness of Volkonsky and Herzen's meeting, described it like this:

"I once visited Herzen and was met by the following picture. An old man is sitting majestically in a large, upholstered chair. He has snow-white shoulder-length hair; his face and body radiate peace, with a hint of the patriarch; his straight, clear look shows his inner conviction of the justice of his cause, and a sense of self-confidence which is only given to people who have lived a long life and have a quiet conscience. Herzen stood in front of the old man, treating him with filial affection of the kind

Anonymous: Portrait of the poet Nikolai Fyodorovich Cherbina. From Aleksei Pyotrovich's Bakhrushin collection. St Petersburg.

Anonymous: The Slakosov
brothers, fireplace-installers
by trade (daguerreotype).
Moscow, c. 1852.

Anonymous: Showing a horse, reproduction of a painting (daguerreotype). This picture illustrates the deterioration to which daguerreotypes are subject. But deterioration can produce an aura: this daguerreotype now seems like a prehistoric cave painting. 1850–1855.

Anonymous: A wealthy woman with her daughter (daguerreotype). C. 1850.

*Martin Abadi: Unidentified
group portrait (daguerreotype). Moscow, c. 1855.*

Alfred Davignon: Grand Duke Sergei Grigorevich Volkonsky, who had been sent to Irkutsk in Siberia as a Decembrist. (This daguerreotype seems to have been tinted only slightly.) Irkutsk, 1845.

Alexander Vassilyevich Drushinin (1824–1864). He was for a time a civil servant in the Ministry of War, then later a freelance writer and critic. Known for his novella *Polinka Sachs* (1843), in which he demands equal rights and personal freedom of women.

that can only be awakened by someone who carries it in his own heart to an even greater extent."

Levitsky caught the nobility, dignity, unbending strength and importance of the famous hero of the December Revolution in his work. The portrait of Herzen is very well known, and is again a tribute to the artistic qualities of the daguerreotype. Herzen himself considered the portrait 'excellent'.

But the most striking feature of Levitsky's work is his portrait gallery of Russian writers. The starting point for this was a portrait of a group of writers who worked on the periodical *Sovre-*

mennik, which gave the ingenious businessman the idea of producing a series of individual portraits. These were taken in Levitsky's studio in St Petersburg in February 1856, and form a separate group, complete in itself, within his oeuvre. The historian M I Semevsky described his impressions of these photographs as follows: "Ostrovsky introduced us to [Levitsky's] photographic studio. We saw the poet Polonsky's blazing stare; the poet Maykov, modest and subtle; Poechin, reminiscent of the hero of his last novel because of the way he held his head; *Drushinin, with his tiny, sparkling eyes, the good-natured author of *Rudin*; Grigorevich with his lorgnette; Pisaemsky, massive, solid, with an open, clear gaze; the young Tolstoy; Ostrovsky himself, with his permanent humourous smile." One of the photographer's aims was to convince his fellow countrymen of something Semyonsky had expressed very clearly: "Long live the artist who is introducing France and Europe to the shining stars of contemporary Russian literature."

This series broke the usual pattern. It was seen as a work of art in its own right, and aroused a great deal of interest among the subjects' relatives and friends, and the general public.

About ten years later another work of photographic art, the *Album of Photographic Portraits of Members of the Imperial Family and Important Russian Personalities* by Denier, was equally successful. The photographer released it in parts in 1865 and 1866. The album contained portraits of members of the imperial family, statesmen and famous personalities in public life, academics, literati, actors, and artists. Denier's portrait gallery is very rich and covers a broad range of styles. His best work is remarkably refined and has a three-dimensional quality—this masterly photographer's artistic hallmarks.

One interesting detail: the HISTORICAL MUSEUM's collection includes work that gives an unusual insight into Denier's creative development: portraits of the same person taken in various settings, from several viewpoints, and with different backgrounds.

As the magazine *Photographer* said at the time, this series was interesting from two points of view: as a portrait of the people concerned, and as an example of the creativity of a photographer "who made his name with entirely genuine works of art." At the time this was praise indeed.

Portraits of painters occupy a special place in Denier's work. He was a graduate of the ACADEMY OF ARTS and participated in the exhibition it organized in 1860. On this basis he made his studio into an artists' salon, encouraging discussions about the future of Russian society and art. The group agreed that taking photographs was a creative process.

A particularly unusual work by Denier is a group portrait of Russian painters taken in 1888. It is not typical of its period, as each person is clearly an individual; at the same time the subjects clearly make up a unit not merely because they are in the same picture, but because the composition reflects their community of interest.

Although Levitsky and Denier are relatively well-known, A Bergner is less so, despite the high quality of his work, of which the HISTORY MUSEUM owns a wide cross-section. He was not of Russian nationality and worked in Russia only for ten years, from 1850 to early 1860, but in this period he became very popular. Many Russian celebrities visited his studio in Moscow: Akhatov and his sons, Satin, *Chomyakov, Muravyev-Karsky, Samarin, Turgenev, members of the Chertkov family, Korsh, Mamontov, and others. Bergner never intended to create a portrait gallery with his stamp upon it; he simply carried out his customers' wishes. But today this photographer's work is considered strikingly creative and highly personal, a series complete in itself.

Many of his photographs could be categorized

as apprentice studies, for example a picture of Akhatov taken in 1856. This is the best-known portrait of the writer. Kramskoy enthused about it in a letter to Tretyakov. In 1857 Bergner took pictures of some Decembrists who had returned from Siberia, including Pushchin, Trubetsky, Muravyev-Apostol, and Batenkov. This material shows precisely how these popular heroes were seen by their contemporaries after thirty years of banishment, and is an irreplaceable historical document.

Works by Levitski, Denier, and Bergner show how photography related to fine art, and how

Alfred Davignon: Grand Duchess Maria Nikolayevna Volkonskaya, who followed her husband into exile in Siberia (daguerreotype). Irkutsk, 1845.

Aleksei Stepanovich Chomyakov (1804–1860). Poet, publicist, historian and religious philosopher. One of the principal "Slavophile" theoreticians. He defended the Eastern church in his theological writings and criticized the denominations of the West.

Right: Sergei Lvovich Le-
vitsky: Portrait of Alexander
Ivanovich Herzen. Paris,
1861.

Left: Martin Abadi: A noble
couple (daguerreotype).
Moscow 1850-1855.

they influenced each other in the second half of the nineteenth century. At first photographers saw fine art as their ideal, then later painters and other visual artists were influenced by photography. One sign of this development was the great use made of photographic materials in fine art. W Timm's montages in the *Russian Art Magazine* and some prints were based on photographs by the artists named, and the same is true of portraits by I N Kramskoy and A Münster's wide-ranging series 'Portrait Gallery of Some Notable Russian Personalities'. Photographers' work was celebrated as a great

event in the cultural life of Russian society. A particularly striking example of this is A O Karelins, described as "our Russian celebrity" in magazines between 1870 and 1880. The HISTORY MUSEUM's collection of photographs by Karelin includes some self-portraits. In several of them he is shown with examples of his own works or with painter's impedimenta—a paintbrush or an easel. As a painter he regarded photography as an inseparable component of the world of art. Many photographers in the last century called themselves 'art photographers'—a designation that fits Karelin perfectly. Objects from antiquity appear with increasing frequency as props and as part of the interior in his late self-portraits, alongside 'artistic' details. He wrote this dedication on one of the originals: "To the esteemed Pyotr Ivanovich Chuykin in kind memory of his devoted A O Karelin. 1894." The address was a well-known collector of antiques who had common interests and business connections with Karelin, who

Andrei I Denier: Group of Russian painters, including Ivan Ivanovich Chishkin, Ilya Yefimovich Repin and Archip Ivanovich Kuindshi, Nikolai Nikolayevich Dubovsky, A A Kiselev, Yefim Yefimovich Volkov, Alexander Karlovich Begrov, V Vasnetsov, N D Kuznetsov, V N Maksimov, L V Pozen, M A Mroshenko, N A Savitsky, V E Mamovsky and N K Bodarevsky. St Petersburg, 1888.

*S Levitsky: S Volkonsky,
Paris, 1861*

began to collect old objets d'art and utensils in 1880. Chyukin writes in his memoirs: "The great hall and the house are reminiscent of an antique shop." The Museum's archive includes letters of Karelin's containing information about ancient utensils, and drawings and photographs of them. Chyukin himself later wrote about the origins of his collection: "My principal supplier was the photographer Andrei Osipovich Karelin." Karelin had a similar relationship with another antique dealer, Barushin. Karelin's work was received with enthusiasm by his contemporaries, and his portraits, the *Art Album of Nature Photography*, the *Nizhni Novgorod Album*, and other works are similarly received today. His style is distinctive because it is so personal. Every page in the *Art Album of Nature Photography* is a work of photographic art, whether it is a genre composition or landscape.

Karelin's group portraits are of particular interest. These are the so-called 'room' groups. The compositions are conceived with great precision, and show such a high degree of spontaneity and naturalness that one forgets that they were staged. The surrounding objects are highly significant, and an everyday interior becomes the background for action. Sometimes it seems that the subjects could spring to life any minute, and start to move and speak. Karelin's genre compositions could be called photographic novellas, painted in light. Before starting work Karelin tried to define his artistic objectives, and then translated them clearly into practice.

The album called *Nizhni Novgorod* is different from the *Art Album of Nature Photography* in that it contains photographs of views and characters which give a precise picture of the town and its surroundings, of the people who live in it and their various social groups. Here, Karelin shows himself to be a connoisseur of Russian architecture with real feeling for his subject: he selects his viewpoints with great cave, photo-

graphs the building from many viewpoints, and highlights architectural details. His camera finds its way into the interior of the cathedrals in Novgorod, where he takes pictures of the interior and religious objects.

Views, characters, and everyday scenes were traditional subjects for Russian photographers. When Stasov pointed out that "photography is a great achievement," he was referring to its ability to reproduce "everything in this world." This aspect of the new invention was immediately applied over a broad range of subjects. Photographers gradually replaced painters on geographical and ethnographic expeditions. Explorers brought photographic material from faraway parts of Russia, and contemporaries were astonished by their rich content and precise reproduction.

Such material was published in special ethnographic albums; there are several of these in the archives of the HISTORY MUSEUM. Bukar's *Album of Photographs of Characters in the Orenburg Region* and Kordysh's *Ethnographic Album of Little Russia* (the Ukraine) are classic examples of early ethnographic work produced in the 1870s.

As the dedication on the title page shows, Bukar wanted to present his album to Alexander II. In order to create as perfect an ethnographic picture as possible, he tinted the photographs, which gave the work a special effect.

Both Bukar and Kordysh staged their photographs to a certain extent. The characters of Little Russia and the Orenburg region, dressed in national costume, are clearly posing like models, surrounded by household utensils, the tools of their trade, and everyday objects.

D J Yermakov developed a new quality in ethnographic photography. His aim was to show provincial life by exploiting special facilities. He equipped a covered wagon as a photographic laboratory and traveled the length and breadth of Armenia, Azerbaijan, and Georgia. His work shows amazing richness and diversity: landscapes, architectural monuments, utensils, people from various tribes and nationalitiles, their practices, their feasts, work, and everyday life.

Yermakov's subjects, posing picturesquely in pavilions with lots of props, or photographed as he found them—in the fields, in workshops, in kiosks, and in the streets of towns and villages—give an insight into the photographer's attitude to his subjects—sometimes affection, sometimes profound compassion, sometimes gentle humor—but the documentary photographer's professional interest is a constant element.

His work includes journalistic photos always jokingly said to have been taken at the scene of the crime: in the streets of Tiflis in the days of unrest in 1905, during fires in the oil fields, after the Azerbaijan earthquake of 1897.

A S Mazurin, an amateur, also took some interesting photographs. Posed genre scenes, pictures of the architectural monuments and of the streets and squares of Moscow, the famous Masurin winter landscapes—they all show a high level of ability. They are to an extent related to Karelin's work, but are in a completely different artistic language.

Mazurin's photographic scenes from the life of the people reflect the interest of photographers in the 1890s in genre photography. Both those who directly imitated fine art and those who tried to find a specifically photographic means of expression created works stamped with a high degree of sympathy and interest in the life of the people.

Formal considerations were sometimes pushed into the background by the objectives of a particular piece of photography. The HISTORY MUSEUM's collection contains a series of photo-

Karl August Bergner: A noblewoman with her children—a classic studio picture of the period. Moscow, 1855–1860.

graphs by Savadsky, a professional photographer working as a correspondent for the magazine *Iskra*, which appeared as a supplement to the newspaper *Russkoye Slovo*. This series was commissioned and produced in Moscow in the uneasy days of the December uprising of 1906. The pictures were produced in extremely complicated conditions. The photographer captured on film the bitter struggles, the groups of revolutionaries, the ruined houses, streets, and squares, and the barricades.

Left: Karl August Bergner: Journalist Aleksei Stepanovich Chomyakov. Moscow, 1855–1860.

Right: Karl August Bergner: The father of the patron Savva Ivanovich Mamontov (studio portrait). Moscow, c. 1855.

Page 55 left: Andrei Andreyevich Karelin: Self-portrait. The photographer with the attributes of the painter. These two arts met in his person. Nizhni Novgorod, c. 1890.

Above: Andrei Andreyevich Karelin: Portrait from Artistic Photographs. *Nizhni Novgorod, 1870–1880.*

Andrei Andreyevich Karelin: Olga Grigoryevna Karelina. Nizhni Novgorod, 1870–1880.

Right: Andrei Andreyevich Karelin: Olga Grigoryevna Karelina, the wife of the photographer, with her daughters. From the album Artistic Photographs. *Nizhni Novgorod, 1870–1880.*

Above right: Andrei Andreyevich Karelin: Carte-de-Visite-Portrait of the Russian writer Vladimir Galaktionovich Korolenko. On the lower edge are some of the numerous medals won by the photographer at exhibitions at home and abroad. Nizhni Novgorod, c. 1890.

Below right: Carte-de-Visite-Portrait of the Russian poet Yakov Polonsky. Nizhni Novgorod, c. 1890.

Andrei Andreyevich Karelin: Page from the album Photographs in natura. *Nizhni Novgorod, 1870–1880.*

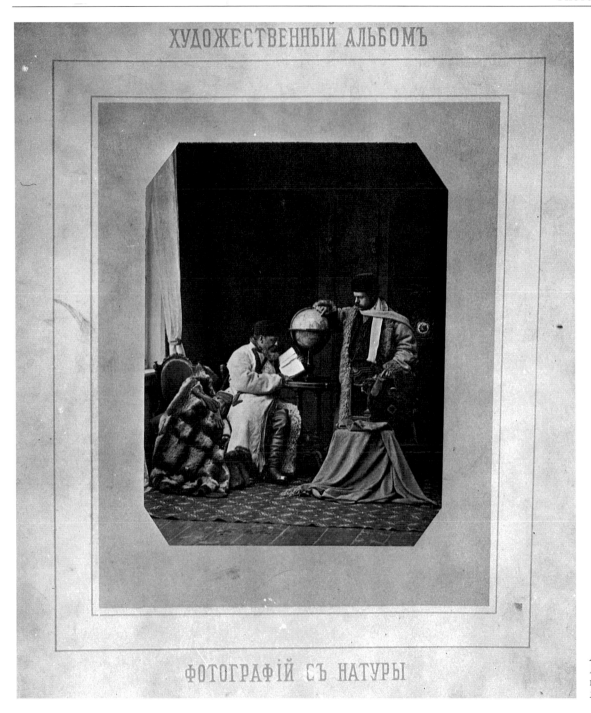

ХУДОЖЕСТВЕННЫЙ АЛЬБОМЪ

ФОТОГРАФІЙ СЪ НАТУРЫ

Andrei Andreyevich Karelin:
Page from Photographs in
natura. *Nizhni Novgorod,*
1870–1880.

Yosif Kordysh: Village musicians. From the Ethnographic Album of Little Russia. *Kiev, 1870–1880.*

Yosif Kordysh: Beggars. From the Ethnographic Album of Little Russia. *Kiev, 1870–1880.*

Above left: Yosif Kordysh: Woman fetching water. From the Ethnographic Album of Little Russia. *Kiev, 1870–1880.*

Above right: Yosif Kordysh: Seventy-year-old bandura player. From the Ethnographic Album of Little Russia. *Kiev, 1870–1880.*

Below left: Dmitri Ivanovich Yermakov: Carpet shop in Maidan, a district of Tbilisi. 1890–1900.

Below right: Aleksei Sergeyevich Mazurin: View of Lyubyanskaya Square in the center of Moscow (now Dzerzhinsky Square). Moscow, c. 1900.

Юрта и Семейство Волостнаго Управителя.   *Казахи.*

Mikhail Bukar: Family of a district administrator outside a yurt (hand-tinted print). From the album Photographs of People in the Orenburg Region. *1872.*

Калмыки.

Mikhail Bukar: Kalmuck couple in national costume (hand-tinted print). From Photographs of People in the Orenburg Region. *1872.*

Ташкенскій Сартъ.

Mikhail Bukar: Uzbek from Tashkent preparing a meal (hand-tinted print). From Photographs of People in the Orenburg Region. *1872.*

Тамарка. Уличной костюмъ.

Mikhail Bukar: Tatar woman
in her ceremonial dress
(hand-tinted print). From
Photographs of People in the
Orenburg Region. 1872.

Уральская Казачья жена.

Mikhail Bukar: Cossack woman from the Urals in national costume (hand-tinted print). From Photographs of People in the Orenburg Region. *1872.*

Radishchev: Village. C. 1900.

Maksim Pyotrovich Dmi-
triev: Hunter. The mount
shows that the photograph
was once in an exhibition.
(From the archives of the
Russian Photographic
Society.) Nizhni Novgorod,
c. 1895.

A countryhouse in winter.
Taken by A Mazurin. From
the archives of the Russian
Photographic Society. Early
20th century. Moscow.

Above: Natalya Nordman: Seller of game birds. The photograph was taken by the wife of the painter Ilya Yefimovich Repin. (From the archives of the Russian Photographic Society.) C. 1900.

Left: Natalya Nordman: Young cobbler. From the archives of the Russian Photographic Society. C. 1900.

Dmitri Ivanovich Yermakov: Prince Ovalyani from the Caucasus. The picture was taken in Yermakov's studio. Tbilisi, c. 1890.

9724. Татарскій костюмъ. Дочь К-зи Лазарева. 664.

Dmitri Ivanovich Yermakov: Princess Lasarev in Tatar costume. The picture was produced in Yermakov's studio. Tbilisi, c. 1890.

Above: Sam Hopewood: Fire in the Metropol Hotel. Moscow, 1905.

Sam Hopewood: Religious procession in Red Square. Moscow, 1905.

Above: Anonymous: Sukharov Square in Mosocw. A wonderful panoramic photograph—a technique of which Russian photographers were complete masters. Moscow, c. 1900.

Aleksei Karlovich Savadsky: Barricades at the corner of Zheleznovskaya Street. All the barricades were set up away from the center of the town. Moscow, 1905.

Yelena V Barchatova

Everyday Pictures for Every Day

The archives of the SALTYKOV-SHCHEDRIN STATE PUBLIC LIBRARY, Leningrad

Mikhail Yevgrafovich Salty-kov (1826–1889). Writer, principally a satirist. Produced precise, sharp views of social conditions in Russia. Close to the "Narodniki". Forcibly removed to Vyatka for disciplinary reasons 1848-56. From 1868-84 active worker and later editor-in-chief of the periodical *Annals of the fatherland (Otecestvennys Tsapiski)*, previously called *Contemporary (Sovremennik)*.

The photographic archive of the SALTYKOV-SHCHEDRIN STATE PUBLIC LIBRARY was established in the second half of the nineteenth century. V V Stasov worked in the library as a voluntary helper from 1856 onwards, and played a vital role in the archive's early development. From 1872 he was in charge of the Department of Art and Technology, which was principally concerned with photography. Its collection consists of individual prints as well as complete albums.

Typically, Stasov's first article, written in 1856 and comparing photography with gravure, showed that he was rare among his contemporaries in having a high opinion of the possible uses of the new discovery. He felt that "the world of art was too remote and unreachable" for photography, and that "it is not for photography to enter into the world of art," but then went on to provide a thorough and incisive analysis of the broader perspectives of photography, which he called "one of the most useful and wonderful inventions . . . and a motor and accelerator for education." Stasov fought many battles for photography in the course of his long creative life.

Stasov constantly allotted tasks to friends and colleagues in the library. In a letter to I P Ropet,

the architect, who was staying in Nizhni Novgorod, he wrote, almost as an aside, "Could you not perhaps take the opportunity of calling on M P Dmitriev, the photographer? . . . I have corresponded with him and he gave me some detailed autobiographical information. . . . As we are a public library perhaps he could sell us the best and most important of his photographs. You know of course that I collect any photographic material concerning Russia in the library here. And his photos of the famine in Nizhni Novgorod—these are extremely important historical data!"

And so the collection acquired a wonderful set of Dmitriev's rare documentary photographs of everyday life by the Volga. The pictures appeared later as a collotype in the album *Scenes from the Failed Harvest of 1891–1892 in Nizhni Novgorod*, which aroused great sympathy in progressive circles. It was thanks to Stasov's efforts that another wonderful "document of the period" was acquired in the form of the album *Views and Characters in Nertshinsk*. Kuznetsov was arrested as a student at the MOSCOW ACADEMY OF AGRICULTURE during the Netshayev Trial and condemned to ten years imprisonment in 1871. While serving his sentence in Transbaikalia, Kuznetsov made a major contribution to ethnographic and historical research in the region. He founded a local-history museum in Nertshinsk and left an interesting photographic legacy.

Stasov was aware of the importance of capturing important contemporary social and cultural events in photographic form. He constantly drew photographers' attention to such subjects, and also commissioned work himself. A collection of photographs by the wonderful Russian photographer and inventor Boldyrev, giving a very full picture of life in Russia between 1870 and 1890, is of extraordinary interest. Here one finds rare photographs of early psychological experiments in *Botkin's clinic at the time that the young Pavlov was working there; of electric-shock treatment in the ST PETERSBURG ACADEMY OF MILITARY MEDICINE; of the celebrations for Raphael's four-hundredth anniversary in the ACADEMY OF ARTS; of the paintings shown in touring exhibitions by the so-called wandering painters.

Boldyrev's extraordinarily varied collection of photographs includes one particular rarity, with a caption by Stasov himself: "I V Boldyrev developing a pitchlike sheet photographic plate. 1878." The photograph shows Boldyrev's fascinating invention of an elastic, transparent negative film to replace fragile glass plates. This invention, sensational for its time, was not exploited commercially in Russia, so that all the praise—and, worse, the copyright—went abroad. This was also the fate of the two-inch long-focal-length lens constructed by Boldyrev and tested by him on a journey to his home in the Don region and in the Crimea, where he used it to take a series of splendid photographs of everyday life in the Cossack settlements of Tsymlyanka, Kumshanka, and Yessaulovka. Stasov was very impressed by these photos, and called them "everday pictures en miniature, drawn by a very talented artist."

But life held little happiness and joy in store for this talented photographic artist. Boldyrev

Yosif Kordysh: Young peasant women. Kiev, 1895.

Sergey Pyotrovich Botkin (1832–1889). He was professor of medicine in St Petersburg from 1861. Co-founder of Russian clinical medicine, and first to build up its study on a scientific basis. He created a new direction for medicine, physiological studies, which was pursued and perfected by Pavlov.

P Ostrovsky: From the album A journey on the Yenisey River. *1894–1897.*

Ivan Vasilyevich Boldyrev:
Photographs from the album
The Palace of Bashiserai.
This photograph, interesting
from an artistic point of
view, has faded with time;
other pictures in the album
are in better condition.

V V Stasov personally en-
couraged him to work on this
album, of which only six
copies were produced. 1880.

Ivan Vasilyevich Boldyrev:
Fair in the Zymlyansky Cos-
sack settlement. 1875/76.

Ivan Vasilyevich Boldyrev:
Sheep-shearing. South-
ukraine, 1875/76.

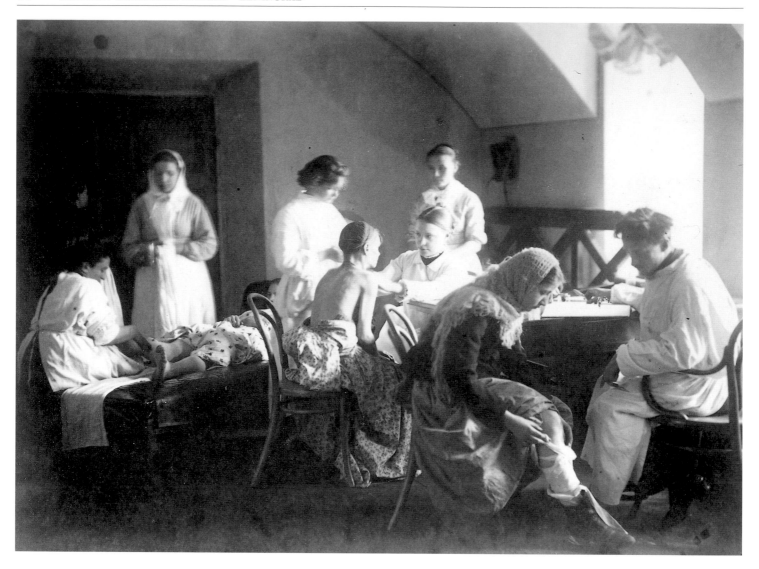

Above: Ivan Vasilyevich Boldyrev: The studio in Obuchov hospital. St Petersburg, 1887.

Right: Ivan Vasilyevich Boldyrev: Professor Sergei Pyotrovich Botkin with pupils in the dissection room. St Petersburg, 1887.

Left: Ivan Vasilyevich Boldyrev: Electrotherapy in the St Petersburg Academy of Military Medicine. 1887.

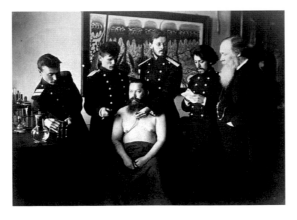

wrote bitterly in 1883: "It is difficult to realize any invention, however useful, if one has no money. Many a useful invention is lost beyond recall in the vastness of Mother Russia." He suffered much and put up with bitter failure, but never saw his technical innovations realized. Boldyrev also constructed an fast shutter that was assessed as "the best of any on the market" at a meeting of the RUSSIAN TECHNICAL SOCIETY in 1889. But, like the shutter invented by Vitebsk photographer Yurkovsky, the prototype of which was introduced in the magazine *Photographer* in 1882, this invention was never produced industrially. The library has an interesting photograph by Yurkovsky dating from 1882 called 'Transporting Part of a Locomotive to the Orlov-Vitebsk Railway Line, Which Was under Construction.' This is an attempt to take a snapshot of a moving object, a very difficult task at the time.

In the catalog *Photographic and Phototype Collections in the Imperial Public Library* which appeared in 1885, Stasov gave a very full description of the rarest and most valuable photographs, which he classified as follows: views, folk characters and portraits, architecture, painting, sculpture, gravure, industrially produced objets d'art. He saw photography as 'rich and inexhaustible medium, of great value to both the academic and the man in the street.' Ethnographic photography became very important in the second half of the nineteenth century. The periodical News of the Russian Geographical Society printed special instructions for photographers in 1872. On the subject of taking ethnographic pictures it said, "Particular attention ... should be paid to people's costume, every single pose, tools and household goods, and also paintings showing the use of any individual object; also dwellings, settlements, towns, etc., various paintings, scenes from public life, and pets."

An example of the application of these principles is the *Turkestan Album*. This is in several

Anonymous: Peasant choir with horn players. A typical genre photograph of the period. One outstanding feature: the musicians' retouched pupils. 1893.

volumes and was prepared in 1871 and 1872 for the governor general; only six copies were produced. It covers every detail of everyday life and traditional crafts in the region, and particular aspects of the geographical conditions under which the people lived. In Stasov's definition the album became "a phenomenon unique of its kind among European works" and "a complete gallery of the people".

Another interesting item is the *Album of Russian Costume*, acquired by the library in 1878. The photographs it contains were commissioned by the MINISTRY OF THE INTERIOR when general conscription was introduced. Costumes from all over the country had been photographed as models for the design of an army uniform in tune with the spirit of the people.

In recent times photographs by Vladimir Andreyevich Karrik have attracted increasing attention. He made an impact with a series on types of road in St Petersburg and the surrounding area. In 1871 he traveled on numerous occa-

*S A Yurkovsky: Transporting
a locomotive to the Orel-Vi-
tebsk railway, then under
construction. The picture is
an early attempt to captur a
moving object on film. Cen-
tralrussia, 1867.*

sions to Simbirsk, where he took photographs of Tatars, Mordovians, and Chuvashes, which earned him the reputation of a master of composition. Karrik took a lot of photographs in Yaroslavl and Tversk. He armed himself with a portable camera, a tent in which he could develop the plates, and a chest containing various chemicals and other equipment. But this artist, who really enriched the fields of photography of everyday life and landscape, actually earned his living as a portrait photographer.

Stasov paid particular attention to the photographic portrait collection, as he knew that such pictures, replacing photogravure, would be a fine addition to the library's collection. This section was always popular with visitors. Some portrait photographs were brought in by photographers, and then bought by the museum, but others were specially commissioned by Stasov. More rarely they appeared by way of censorship committees. Stasov identified a

A L Vishnevsky: Women cutting up fish. 1870–1880.

РѢЗАЛЬЩИЦЫ РЫБАЧКИ.

A L Vishnevsky: Producing salt at Lake Baskundshak in southern Russia. (Saltykov-Shchedrin Public Library.) 1870–1880.

Nikolai Andreyevich Rimsky-Korsakov (1844–1908). Composer, music teacher and conductor. Used popular and imaginative motifs. Composed fourteen operas, three symphonies, symphonic poems, ballet music, choral works, suites and songs. Also known for his works on musical theory and his gifts as a teacher.

need to collect photos which were informative about contemporary life, such as pictures of *Rimski-Korsakov's drawing room or the sculptor Grinzburg's workshop, as well as portraits of well-known personalities in public life—literary figures, musicians and artists.

The public library's photographic archive is an irreplaceable source of material for academic historians and ethnologists, restorers and filmmakers, local historians and museum workers.

It also provides a survey of the development of Russian photography and the way it became an art in its own right, a status it has ever since maintained. Russian photographers were active champions of this cause.

Vladimir Andreyevich Karrik: Group of Finnish peasants. Finland, 1870–1880.

Anonymous: Russian metal-chasers. These men are masters of the old Russian craft of manufacturing samovars and decorating metal objects. Middle Russia (?), 1880–1890.

Yemelyanov: From the album
Life and Everyday Events of
the Mari People. *1880–1890.*

Переселенцы на р. Шилкѣ.

Anonymous: Settlers on the Shilka River in the Urals. People moved east in search of better land. At this time increasing numbers of industrial concerns were being established in the Urals, and they too required workers. 1880–1890.

ТИПЫ НАРОДНОСТЕЙ
СРЕДНЕЙ АЗІИ.

Каракиргизъ 48 л.

Фотогр. В. Козловскаго въ Ташкентъ.

*V Koslovsky: Karakirghiz,
forty-eight years old. From
the album* Peoples of Central
Asia. *Tashkent, 1876.*

ТИПЫ НАРОДНОСТЕЙ
СРЕДНЕЙ АЗІИ.

Сартянка 15 л.

Фотогр. В. Козловскаго въ Ташкентъ.

V Koslovsky: Girl, fifteen years old. From Peoples of Central Asia. *Tashkent 1876.*

МОСКВА.   MOSCOU.

ВИДЪ ИЗЪ ДВОРЦОВАГО САДА НА ХРАМЪ ХРИСТА СПАСИТЕЛЯ   VUE DU TEMPLE DU SAUVEUR, PRISE DU JARDIN DU PALAIS.

Photo-studio Kiriakov (Vol-
chonka Street): View from
the palace park of the Cathe-
dral of Christ the Redeemer.
In the foreground is one of
the towers of the Kremlin.
Moscow, 1870–1880.

Anonymous: View of the Kremlin. On the left is the Ivan the Great bell tower; in front of it is "Tsar Kolokol", the largest bell in the world. In the foreground is the "first nameless tower", which is built into the Kremlin wall behind which is the narrow Kremlin garden. The dome on the right tops the building in which the Soviet Council of Ministers now meets. Moscow, 1870–1880.

*Anonymous: A country pic-
nic of Grand Duchess Maria
Pavlovna. 1913.*

Anonymous: A country picnic of Grand Duchess Maria Pavlovna. 1913.

Karl Karlovich Bulla: Grigori Rasputin with friends. From the album Chronicle of St Petersburg Life. *St Petersburg, c. 1915.*

K E Hahn: Carskoye Selo, the Romanovs' summer residence near St Petersburg. It is a little spa that also contained the grammar school attended by Pushkin. 1902.

Karl Karlovich Bulla: The photographer labeled this picture "terror attack". This is a typical early press photograph. From the album Chronicle of St Petersburg Life. *St Petersburg, 1910.*

Karl Karlovich Bulla: Demonstration by the women regiment on Nevsky Prospekt. St Petersburg, April 1917.

Karl Karlovich Bulla: Alex-
ander Kerensky, the leader of
the provisional government,
with troops. St Petersburg,
1917.

Karl Karlovich Bulla: The women's death battallion. St Petersburg, 1917.

Galina A Mirolubova
Tatyana A Petrova

The Golden Age of Photography

The collection of the HERMITAGE STATE MUSEUM, Leningrad

The Department of 'Russian Cultural History' of the HERMITAGE has an interesting photographic collection. Its forty thousand photographs reflect every stage of the development of the art in Russia and introduce the visitor to a wide range of topics and subjects and the work of outstanding artists and studios. The photography section's proximity to other collections in the HERMITAGE makes it a particularly useful aid to study, giving an impression of the spirit and character of the periods it covers.

The photographic collection was built up in parallel to the main archive of the 'Department of Russian Cultural History'. This department, established in the HERMITAGE in 1941, was based on stock from the 'Department of Historical Articles for Daily Use' in the RUSSIAN STATE MUSEUM. After the October Revolution of 1917, art treasures and articles for everyday use from aristocratic palaces in St Petersburg were brought here after being seized by the state. A large number of photographs, an essential part of every aristocratic household, were found in the palace libraries of the Bobrinsky, Cheremetyev, Chuvalov, Yusupov, Stroganov, and Levashov families; most of these collections had been put together carefully. Large numbers of old photographs were found in the libraries,

studies, and boudoirs of the Winter Palace—the gifts of foreign guests on state visits, arranged by subject in magnificently designed albums. The photographic archive of the museum was founded on the basis of all these sources in the twenties, and then enlarged in the fifties by the addition of photographs from the STATE MUSEUM OF ETHNOGRAPHY OF THE PEOPLES OF THE USSR and the STATE MUSEUM OF THE GREAT SOCIALIST OCTOBER REVOLUTION.

The HERMITAGE collection is dominated by portrait photographs. A hundred and twenty of the many thousands of photographs stand out particularly. These are the daguerreotypes, most of them works by unknown masters who captured their contemporaries by means of 'light pictures' on metal plates covered with a layer of silver. These daguerreotypes are small, set in leather or velvet cases and bronze or wooden frames, they are reminiscent of traditional painted miniature portraits, intended to be kept by the subject or as a present for friends and relations. Only one miniature can be made from each daguerreotype exposure, and they are thus unique.

Some of the daguerreotypes in the HERMITAGE, taken about 150 years ago, have deteriorated. Multicolored patches of oxide have formed on some of the plates, and the image has faded on others. Nevertheless most show a high level of artistic achievement: astonishing liveliness of facial expression, usually accompanied by precise reproduction of detail in the subject's clothes and in the background.

Particularly excellent are the five portrait daguerreotypes of the three sons of Count Bobrinsky—Vladimir, Aleksei and Alexander Alexandreyevich. Their pictures were taken when they were students at the University of St Petersburg, each with the same background: in a room, at a table with a plant on it. The daguerreotypes are all the same size, and outstanding in their sharpness and gentle, refined reproduction both of the young men's features and the detail of their modest surroundings. Original notes on the labels pasted on the back tell us that the pictures date from 1842, and were taken in the first St Petersburg daguerreotype studio set up by I Weinger—suggesting that the count and his family were not merely interested in the new process, but enthusiastic devotees. Their villa in Galernaya Street contained a collection of extremely interesting photographs.

Also very interesting is a potrait daguerreotype of a young girl taken in Rome in 1884. The background is a painted landscape and an ancient column. This is from the personal collection of the famous nineteenth-century Russian photographer Levitsky, who had studied photographic technique in Paris and Italy, and opened a studio in 1851 at 3 Kazankaya Street (opposite Kazan Cathedral). This daguerreotype was probably kept by the Levitsky family as a memento of his early photographic career in Italy, where the first portrait daguerreotype of a group of Russian artists (including Gogol) was taken in 1845.

Another pioneer of Russian photography was A I Denier, also active in St Petersburg from 1850. Denier trained as a painter at the ACADEMY OF ARTS and became very enthusiastic

about photography. He very rapidly became known as a master of the art of the portrait. His career started at a time when the simpler, faster, and cheaper damp collodion photographic process already existed. This made it possible to use paper, which considerably simplified the process, as well as making it cheaper. One of Denier's best early works has survived at the HERMITAGE: a portrait of a young woman, astonishing delicately tinted with water colors by the photographer himself, as the signature and date on the lower part of the picture show. Denier established his reputation with his *Photographic Album with Portraits of Famous Rus-*

I Weinger: Vladimir Count Bobrinsky (ferrotype). 1849.

Anonymous: Vladimir Count Bobrinsky (daguerreotype). Paris, 1844.

clients. Democratic ideas were starting to spread in Russian society, with consequent parallel effects in the world of art, and so their customers were not just members of the Tsar's family or other aristocrats, but also included intellectual commoners, merchants, members of the middle class and, servants.

Pictures by these two St Petersburg photographers, without doubt the best in the city at the time, were always of the highest technical quality, but had no distinctive personal features. Both men composed their pictures in exactly the same way, using the same props, and offering their customers the choice of either a magnificent interior or an equally splendid landscape as a background. Portraits were framed, glazed, and placed on their subjects' walls or tables. Some of them, with dedications giving sparse but valuable, historical information, were sent to friends and relations elsewhere, sometimes over considerable distances.

Almost half the photographs in the HERMITAGE collection came from splendidly designed family albums. This method of collecting photographs was just as popular from the mid-nineteenth century as albums of drawings or poems had been in the early Pushkin period. They were bound in leather or morocco, stamped in gilt, with silver locks and inlays of ivory, semiprecious stones, or malachite. They were kept in separately made covers or cases, and formed part of the domestic reliquary, passed down to the younger members of the family, often with additional photos.

Generally speaking these albums contained portraits taken in the top photographic studios. Less frequently they are the work of amateur photographers. These were less elaborately presented, but are still striking because of the situations they capture and their unstudied poses. They give an impression of many of the subtler shades in the quality of life at that time. From the mid-nineteenth century, photographs were part of everyday Russian life, and indis-

sian Personalities, compiled in 1865. He was also responsible for the best portraits of Fyodor Ivanovich Tyutchev and Tarras Grigoryevich Chevchenko. Denier's portraits were masterly in their technique, and also gave an insight into the sitter's psychology, thus bringing photography closer to painting and drawing.

Denier was a skillful photographer, but by no means as productive as many of his colleagues. S L Levitsky's photographic studio enjoyed its greatest popularity from 1860 to 1880. From 1867 he worked with his son and Charles Bergamasco. Levitsky and Bergamasco were court photographers, both with a wide circle of

*M Stohl (?): Portrait of a
girl. This daguerreotype was
brought back as a souvenir of
Italy by the subsequently
famous photographer Sergei
Lvovich Levitsky. Both the
picture and its condition are
extraordinary. Rome, 1848.*

*Anonymous: Grand Duchess
Maria Nikolayevna (daguerreotype). C. 1840.*

*Anonymous: Daguerreotype
of an unknown woman.
1850–1859.*

*Charles Bergamasco:
Daguerreotype of Grand
Duchess Maria Alexan-
drovna. 1860–1870.*

Above: Andrei I Denier: Princess Dashkova. 1864.

Above left: A Bernhard: Daguerreotype portrait of Princess S Volkonskaya (tinted with ink and white color). C. 1850.

Below left: Anonymous: Daguerreotype portrait of an unknown woman (tinted with water color). 1860–1870.

Anonymous: Portraits in a pull-out album kept in a decorated wooden case. 1870–1885.

pensable in interior design, on a par with paintings and watercolors. This phenomenon can be studied in detail in the interior of the Novo-Mikhailovsky grand-ducal palace in St Petersburg. On the desk in the study are lamps, a clock, and writing materials, then a large number of fold-out photographs, more of which can be seen on the smaller pieces of furniture. All these photographs and other objects make the interior seem somewhat cluttered for modern tastes, and give the impression that the occupant is about to move house, or at least redecorate. Groups of photographs formed compositions in their own right, and were sometimes the most important feature on the walls in the entire room. One such wall in the Novo-Mikhailovsky Palace became a veritable photographic 'iconostasis'.

The rooms in the Levachovs' house on the Fontanka also remind us of the important role of photographs in the late-nineteenth-century domestic interior. In the music room, photographed in 1885 by an unknown artist, there is furniture of every possible shape and style, vases and books stand on a semicircular shelf, and on the wall are a set of antlers, paintings and framed photographs.

Photographs of fine buildings that no longer exist are invaluable. Pictures taken by the Moscow firm of Scherer and Nabgolz in the late nineteenth century show famous rooms in the great Kremlin and Term palaces, but also rooms that have not survived, such as the Andreyev room in the great palace of the Kremlin with its massive pylons, pilasters with decorated capitals, frieze with medallions, and magnificent gilded ceiling ornaments. The Alexander room is similar, with high plinthed columns with spiral stucco decoration. The vault shone with starlike medallions, and the walls carried scenes from the life of Alexander Nevsky. Photographs of these magnificent rooms give an idea of how state rooms were decorated in this palace built in the 1840s by the architect Ton.

At the turn of the century a new genre was born: photographic reportage, and here the great master was K K Bulla. He turned his attention to life in the town and its architectural monuments, epoch-making and ordinary events, everyday life, the people's occupations, and traffic, but above all the Nevsky Prospekt: Bulla's photographs of this street give us many interesting views of the architecture and everyday life of the times. A view of the 'Gostiny Dvor' department store with its large central dome, urns and sculptures on the roof, and carved columns will come as something of a surprise to visitors to modern Leningrad. All this was the result of the 'beautification' of 'Gostiny Dvor' by Benois in the eighteen-eighties, on the occasion of the building's hundredth anniversary. It was restored to its old form in the 1940s.

Above left: Mikhail P Nastyukov: A businessman's wife. 1865.

Above right: K Anderson: A businessman's wife. 1860–1870

Below right: Suskipi: Princess Lopuchina-Demidova. 1860–1870.

Mikhail P Nastyukov: Docks
in the town of Kalyazin on
the Volga in the province
Tver. 1867.

Mikhail P Nastyukov: The Volga quay in Rybinsk in the province Jaroslavl. 1867.

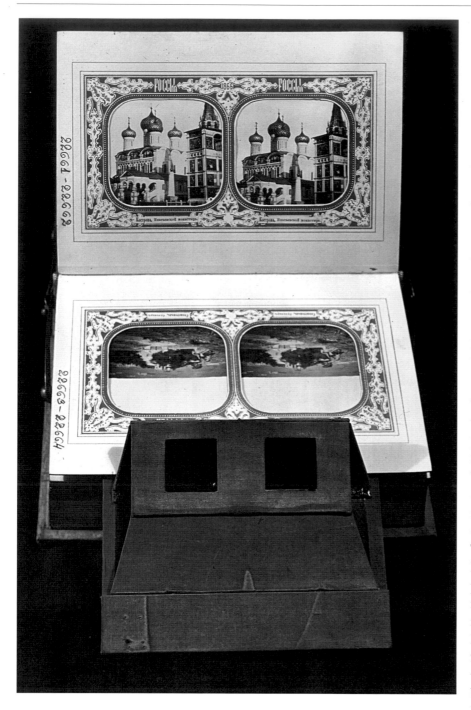

K K Bulla also photographed journeys on Leningrad's first trams. One of the earliest and most important lines ran along the Nevsky Prospekt to the Winter Palace, then onward via Eight-Line Street on Vassily Island. Bulla also took pictures of the first iron bridge over the Neva, the Nikolayevsky Bridge, showing a characteristic early-twentieth-century view of the road along the banks of Vassily Island, steamers and sail boats at the landing stage, workers hurrying to and fro, horse-trams, and a chapel that no longer exists.

K K Bulla used often to visit the outlying districts of Leningrad. This is why events like the Easter Market in Pokrovskaya Square (now Turgenev Square) or the Carnival on the Diversion Canal have been preserved for posterity in photographs: the latter shows a huge crowd of people in an enormous area, enjoying theater, helter-skelters, photographers' stands, and auctions.

The fairground booths outside the Admiralty, which were always set up in Easter Week, were photographed by A Lorens. After popular carnivals moved from Admiralty Square to the Tsar's Field (now Champ de Mars), the Alexander Gardens were planted near the Admiralty, which changed the appearance of this part of the city considerably.

There is a whole series of 'city portraits' of unknown authorship. These include a masterly photograph of an interesting panorama including the Winter Palace, and a series showing the newly opened Peter the Great Bridge over the Neva (Bolsheochinsky Bridge), built between 1908 and 1911. The same series includes a picture of the handsome silhouette of the last bridge built over the Neva before the October Revolution, with the broad river in the background.

The HERMITAGE collection is eloquent testimony to the high degree of interest in landscape photography in the early years. There is even a series of photographs dating from the daguer-

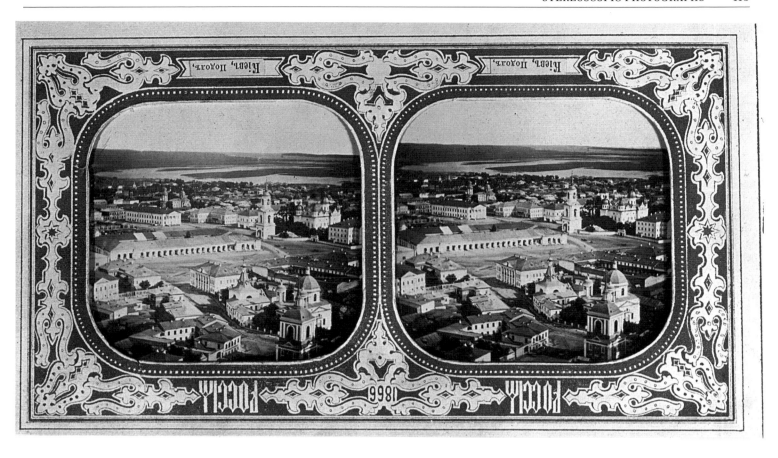

*A Vladsky: Panorama of the
Kiev suburb of Podol. From*
Pictures from Russia in 1866.
Kiev, 1866.

*Page 112: A Vladsky: Stereo-
graphs from the album* Pictures from Russia in 1866. *In
the foreground is the device
for viewing stereoscopic pictures. The picture above
shows a church in Kostroma,
below (upside down) a picture from Sevastopol. 1866.*

Vladimir Vysotsky: Portrait of Madame Gudim. On the right is Vysotsky's graphically outstanding carte-de-visite. Kiev, 1875–1885.

Vladimir Vysotsky: Portrait of Madame Gudim. On the right is Vysotsky's graphically outstanding carte-de-visite. Kiev, 1875–1885.

reotype era, but problems with light and compositional difficulties meant that a lot of these well-intentioned attempts failed. Numerous albums of landscape photographs appeared from the mid-nineteenth century onwards. Among the most significant of these is the album of *Views of Places on the Volga from Tver to Kazan, Taken by the Moscow Photographer MP Nastyukov in 1867.* The picturesque banks of the Volga have attracted artists from time immemorial. Photographers took a leaf out of the painters' book and produced photographic 'portraits' of the famous river, work of great documentary value. Great masters, including Nastyukov, took outstanding pictures. His album includes Volga landscapes and town views, for example the well-known Ipatyevsky monastery in Kostroma and the monument to Ivan Zu-

zanin there, and the cathedral in Rybinsk. There is also an interesting photograph of a famous bell tower in the town of Kalatsin. The tower was destroyed by floods while the Volga-Baltic Canal was being built.

Less well known is the name of the author of an album entitled *Views of Russia in 1866—Stereoscopic Views Taken by the Outstanding Painter A Vladsky.* This small album (21 x 14cm) is in a special case with a beautifully designed ivory lid. Each page contains two photographs arranged in such a way as to give a three-dimensional effect when viewed through a stereoscope. Vladsky took photographs of Kiev, many Crimean towns, Rostov on the Don, and the cities of the Volga. The album is a mixture of photographs of buildings, landscapes, and panoramic views of towns.

Anonymous: Interiors in the Levashovs' house on the Fontanka River. St Petersburg, 1885.

M Greym: Pages from the album Photos from Podolsk and Bessarabia. *1889.*

Photographers were attracted to people's faces in Russia's many regions, as well as landscapes. One of the first such collections is in the HERMITAGE, an album assembled by Greym in Kamenets-Podolsky and presented to the IMPERIAL GEOGRAPHICAL SOCIETY in 1889 on the occasion of the fiftieth anniversary of photography. The album contains 175 photographs of Bessarabian peasants, craftsmen, beggars, middle-class citizens, Polish intellectuals and, Jews. The pictures are very static, suggesting that the photographer was concerned more with composing a group or a scene than presenting an objective reproduction of characteristic ethnographical features. Even so, these photographs are a priceless document because of the sharp representation of faces, clothing, and typical surroundings.

In the late nineteenth century, albums devoted

Above: V Dossekin: Two women by a window. 1870–1880.

Left: A Vasilyev: Portrait of S Vereshagina. 1890–1900.

Page 118/119: Karl Karlovich Bulla: View of Nevsky Prospekt with the State Duma (left) and shopping arcades (right). St Petersburg, c. 1906.

Karl Karlovich Bulla: Ceremonial opening of the tram service. St Petersburg, c. 1906.

to private events began to appear. An example of this is *Open-Air Theater on Olga Island in 1897*, an album put together by the Imperial Theater photographer, V Petrov. Pictures of various parts of Olga Island appear on the dark-green background of the album pages, gleaming and picturesque.

From the mid-nineteenth century the Petershof Park and quite frequently Olga Island itself were the setting for various festivities, often including open-air theatrical performances with magnificent colored lighting effects. An open-air theater in the shape of an ancient ruin had been built on the island. The main entrance was a half-ruined portico, in front of which 'ancient' sconces and a statue of Venus had been set up. Inside the 'ruined walls' was a spacious stand for spectators. Pavilions by the Olga and Tsaritsin lakes served as backdrops for the theatrical performances, along with the lush green of the island parks and the lakeside. Petrov's album

presents one aspect of the history of the park and is of particular interest now: restoration work is in hand, as all the buildings on the Great Olga Island and in the Petershof Park were badly damaged in the Second World War.

Photo albums in the late nineteenth and early twentieth centuries are a valuable recored of the construction of factories, mines, stations, and railways. Many albums were devoted to industrial exhibitions—local, international, or embracing the whole of Russia.

In 1885 the 'First Moscow Craft Exhibition' took place in Moscow. This event attracted the attention of Gribov, who had a photographic studio in Volchonka Street, near the Christus-Spatsiten Church. His album shows every aspect of the exhibition, including many of the exhibits: clothing, hats, dolls, umbrellas, furs, metal products, lamps, woodcarvings, and harness for horses.

Inevitably, photographers were attracted to the

great 'Pan-Russian Exhibition' in Nizhni Novgorod in 1896. The distinguished M P Dmitriev was invited to be chief photographer, and his work was shown there. He photographed the opening of the exhibition, and the interior and exterior of the pavilions. Some of Dmitriev's work at the Nizhni Novgorod exhibition is in the HERMITAGE collection, and of high technical quality, showing the photographer's ability to find the right viewpoint from which to capture all the characteristics of a pavilion's design and at the same time to present the architectural background in a lively fashion. It is hardly surprising that his work won many prizes at international photographic exhibitions.

K K Bulla also photographed exhibitions early in the century. His photographs include exhibits by the famous St Petersburg jewelery firm of Fabergé—fans, clocks, cases, and figures decorated with semiprecious stones, the property of Tsarina Alexandra Fedorovna and her relations.

The HERMITAGE collection gives a view of the development of photography from 1840 to the early years of the twentieth century, showing clearly the close correlation between photography and painting in those early years. Yet again it is clear that the work of the great photographers was art; it has continued to attract interest, and has become an important subject for research.

Above: A Lorens: Booths at the fair in Easter week in Admiralty Square. St Petersburg, c. 1895.

Below: Anonymous: Opening of the Peter the Great Bridge. St Petersburg, 1911.

Anonymous: Panoramic view
across the Neva to the Winter
Palace (panoramic photo-
graph). It was a specialty of
Russian photographers to
handle panoramic cameras
confidently. St Petersburg,
c. 1906.

Page 124/125: Karl Karlovich Bulla: Festival on the water-diversion canal. St Petersburg, c. 1908.

Page 126/127: Karl Karlovich Bulla: View of a quay on the Neva by the Nikolai Bridge. St Petersburg, c. 1908.

*Karl Karlovich Bulla: Tolstoy
riding. Yasnaya Polyana,
1908 (?).*

Karl Karlovich Bulla: Tolstoy with his family outside his house in Yasnaya Polyana. On his right is his wife Sofya Andreyevna Tolstaya, who was an enthusiastic amateur photographer. 1908 (?).

Unknown amateur photog-
rapher: Two double pages
from a family album. C.1900.

Ebba Norkute

The Photographer and His Majesty the Theater

The collection of the STATE MUSEUM FOR THEATER AND MUSIC, Leningrad

Karl Karlovich Bulla: Portrait of the opera singer R Gorskaya, who appeared at the Marinsky Theater. St Petersburg, 1916.

This chapter presents photographs from the collection of the Leningrad STATE MUSEUM FOR THEATER AND MUSIC, many of them of famous actors. Each photograph is typical of its period, showing not just the actor's personality, but also giving an impression of the beauty and spirit of the age.

Theatrical photography was not widespread in Russia until the second half of the nineteenth century. In the 1860s there were photographic studios in St Petersburg whose services were used by actors at the municipal theater. Bergamasco, Denier, Levitsky, and Lorens were the best-known of the photographers who settled in smart quarters of St Petersburg: on the Nevsky Prospekt, in the Bolshaya, the Malaya Morskaya Uliza, and on the Moika Embankment.

The large number of surviving theatrical photographs shows that even 'second-class actors', members of the *corps de ballet*, and even impoverished supernumeraries could afford such pictures. It is however perfectly possible that they attempted to supplement their low incomes by duplicating the photographs and selling them in shops. We must also acknowledge

the paradoxical yet understandable fact that the worse an actor was, the more photographs he had taken. The fact that there are few photographs of actors in particularly successful roles is probably because these celebrities didn't see themselves as particularly important, and gave scant thought to future theatrical historians.

Also actors were put off by the fiddly procedure involved in taking photographs and the difficulties of capturing the dynamics of stage presentation. But many talented actors did not think much of the whole business. Yermolova said that a picture of her in the role of Joan of Arc looked like 'a gendarme in a skirt', and M G Savina wrote on one of her portraits: 'subaltern on parade'.

Photographers, though, were always interested in actors as models. They appeal because of their naturalness, their style and quirks, their body language, their expressiveness, and of course their ability to remain in full command before the public and to slip rapidly into a different role. It is interesting however that early Russian theatrical photographers did not concentrate on the actors' natural qualities, nor on those acquired through the profession: the photographers were distinguished by a certain lack of refinement. Accessories, pose, and angle are almost always the same, so if we are able to draw any conclusions about the character, feelings, and taste of the person portrayed from photographs of this kind, it is a kind of accidental 'photographic miracle'. We must assume that in these rare cases the genuine affection and respect of photographer for model helped to make the personality to seem natural and unaffected.

Differences in social position did not affect photographer or subject at all. A portrait of a dancer in the early stages of her career could be just as attractive as a portrait of a prima ballerina, a great beauty, or a court favorite, and a picture of an unsuccessful actor could be as revealing as that of a famous performer in human terms.

Photographers used to stick a label on the back of their photographs. This carried their name and address, and also a list of awards won and important places the photographer had worked. Thus we learn that Charles Bergamasco won awards at exhibitions in Berlin in 1865, Hamburg in 1868, and St Petersburg in 1870, and was photographer at the courts of Grand Duke Nikolai Nikolayevich the Elder, the Prince of Wales, German and Prussian princesses, and Archduke Albert of Austria. But really he offered long, faithful, and devoted service to one titled personage, and one only—His Majesty the Theater.

In the late 1860s the first tinted photographs appeared. In technique they were reminiscent of elegant miniatures, prepared with great mastery. Unfortunately the secrets of their production and names of the artists responsible are unknown. We can only assume that some of them were colored by the photographers themselves, as masters such as Denier and Bergamasco had studied at the ACADEMY OF ARTS.

Andrei I Denier: Teacher from the ballet department of the theater school. St Petersburg, 1872.

Page 134: Charles Bergamasco: M Slavina as Carmen in Bizet's opera, which has been performed at the Marinsky Theater. St Petersburg, 1885.

Archip Ivanovich Kuindshi (1842–1910). Landscape painter and pupil of Ayvazovsky. Member of the "Peredvishniky". Got to know early Expressionism in Paris.

Some tinted photographs dating from the 1880s were actually signed by Bergamasco, but the technique was different from that used in the 1860s.

It is known that Denier persuaded talented young painters such as I Kramskoy, Mikhail Alexandrovich Zishi and Archip Ivanovich Kuindshi to work in his studio, but the practice of coloring photographs using the techniques of the miniature did not persist for long. This was probably because the procedure was very laborious, and therefore expensive. Mass demand for photographs thus put an end to an interesting experiment.

The choice of subject for 'color photography' is interesting. The principal models were singers in operatic costume and a few ballerinas. As almost no designs for theatrical costumes have survived from the 1850s, tinted photographs by Levitsky, Bergamasco, Lorens, and Denier are of considerable interest, but it is doubtful whether they are reliable documents. It quite frequently happens that the same theatrical costume is colored differently on different photographs. Photography begins to loose its unique documentary status, and becomes more like applied art.

In the late nineteenth century the state also started to take an interest in photography: in 1890 a photographic studio for the IMPERIAL THEATER was set up on three floors of the right wing of the Marinsky Theater. The rooms were arranged thoughtfully and practically—there was even a room "for the costuming of actors." The staff was also ideally composed: a photographer, two copiers, three retouchers for positives, three retouchers for negatives, a bookbinder, a lacquerer, four apprentices, an attendant, and a female clerk.

The studio worked for the IMPERIAL THEATER group. It existed for one and a half years, during which it produced 5,000 negatives and 3,000 positives. Photographs were taken of theater auditoria and foyers, the various workshops, an enormous number and variety of sets, moldings, actors and other staff, rooms in the drama school, coachhouses, etc. The administration's relationship with the studio was extremely positive, but they were interested in only one of the aspects of this activity: they thought it desirable "to preserve ideas of acting and make-up" of the actors and wanted "better backstage administration and an accurate inventory, thus obviating the necessity of sorting through a hundred things in the storerooms to find a particular object." A directive of this kind was unlikely to have been received with any great enthusiasm as a stimulus to expressive creativity. In fact the IMPERIAL THEATER proved unfruitful ground for artistic work. The high-flown scheme soon collapsed, and the photographers looked for more satisfying work elsewhere.

Despite all this, theatrical photography clearly developed into an art towards the end of the nineteenth century. Thanks to photographers' efforts, talent, and the profound sense of beauty that many of them had, it was possible to work around the adminstration's prescriptions, and even photographers directly responsible to the directors of the IMPERIAL THEATER did this. But actors increasingly sought out photographers for themselves, to suit their character and personal taste.

Krzesinska, for example, usually had her photographs taken in the theater studio, and did not bother with a personal photographer. A young actor called Yuriev was not looking for talent, but posed for photographers simply because it was his duty. Very few photographs of him have survived, and by no means all of those convey the young artist's creative talent.

Anna *Pavlova liked having her photograph taken. She sat for many photographers, and it is not clear whether she preferred one in particular. Thus there are many photographs of Pavlova, all of very different standards, according to the particular artist—but she is beautiful on all of them! V F Komissarshevskaya also had

Charles Bergamasco: Maria Mariusovna Petipa, a famous dancer at the Marinsky Theater in the opera "The Enchanted Wood" by Drigo. She was so popular that her portrait appeared on soap packaging. St Petersburg, 1887.

Anonymous: Opera singers at the theater in St Petersburg. In the photographs the costumes were magnificently tinted—not always in the true colors. This bending of the truth in no way detracts from the beauty of the costumes, however. St Petersburg, c. 1870.

Anna Pavlovna Pavlova (1885–1931). She entered the Imperial Ballet School in St Petersburg in 1891, joined the Marinsky Theater in St Petersburg in 1899, and became its prima ballerina in 1906. In 1905 she created Fokine's "Dying Swan", which made her world-famous. She undertook triumphant foreign tours. From 1909–1911 she was a member of the Ballets Russes and partnered Nijinsky. She is one of the most important exponents of classical ballet. Caught abroad when the First World War broke out, she did not return to Russia after the 1917 Revolution.

Page 137: The opera singers portrayed on this page all appeared at the Grand Theater in St Petersburg. The pictures are by some of the most famous photographers in the capital, like Charles Bergamasco and A Lorens. Above left J Platonova as Valentine in Giacomo Meyerbeer's "The Huguenots". St Petersburg.

BERGAMASCO PHOT

Левицкій
на Мойкѣ 30 С.Петербургъ.

Левицкій
на Мойкѣ 30 С.Петербургъ.

ALFRED LORENS   S. PETERSBOURG

Левицкій
на Мойкѣ 30 С.Петербургъ.

ALFRED LORENS   S. PETERSBOURG

Yelena Mrozovskaya: This tableau shows extraordinary work by the only female theater photographer: her pictures showed the actors almost in action. This is M I Dolina as Vanya in Glinka's opera "The Life of the Tsar", presented at the Marinsky Theater. St Petersburg.

*Charles Bergamasco: Dancer
at the Grand Theater.
St Petersburg, 1880–1890.*

Above: Anonymous: Pages from a two-volume boxed album. The two pictures on the left show Sarah Bernhardt, on the right beside her Lev Nikolayevich Tolstoy and on the extreme right the historian Vladimir Solovev. C. 1890.

Right: Anonymous: Pupil at the theater-school ballet class. A picture from the Imperial Theater's photographic studio. St Petersburg, c. 1888.

photographs taken very frequently. Before she went on tour or appeared in the capital she wanted to be sure that various aspects of her roles had been captured.

In the early twentieth century, the most popular theatrical photographers in St Petersburg were Renz, Schreder, Lorens, Wesenberg, Pasetti, Belyavsky, and Perl, all with established studios. St Petersburg actors sometimes used photographers like Skassi and Ivanitsky of Kharkov, and Shapiro, Steinberg, Ocup, and K K Bulla also worked with actors a lot. It was at this time that theater photography started to reach large numbers of people: whole series of picture postcards were published, the best-known from negatives by Fischer and Bystrov.

Yelena Mrozovskaya occupied a particular place among early-twentieth-century theater photographers. Even though she hardly figures in the history of photography she has a claim to be called the first truly theatrical photographer in St Petersburg. She arranged her photographs in such a way that the camera appeared to see the actor from the point of view of the theatergoer in the auditorium. She lit the model as if he were on the stage, which gave a three-dimensional effect and emphasized the features. Mrozovs-

Left: Andrei I Denier: Russian poetess Sinaida Gippius with art historian and ballet critic A Volynsky. 1890–1895.

Right: Konstantin Shapiro: Violinist I Pikkel and composers E Naprovnik and K Liadov. The stamp under this studio picture shows, as was quite common, the photographer's address in Cyrillic and Latin characters. St Petersburg, c. 1860.

kaya's photographs give a sense of the space affected by the actor's body language.

The cinematograph had hardly been invented when Mrozovskaya hit on the notion of photographic strips showing details of actors in their roles. Similar experiments had been conducted before, but as exposure techniques were at an early stage in their development the effect was not the same. From the earliest days of photography until the 1930s, photographers followed the techniques and precepts of pictorial art. Mrozovskaya was a modern photographer, and took many pictures of actors under the influence of the Secession, Art Nouveau, and the Modern movement: outstanding, skillfully exposed portraits.

Mrozovskaya was oblivious to styles used before she came on the scene. She was not producing simple, entertaining salon pictures; every pho-

tograph was based on a particular idea, a concept. Some portraits showed femininity and unusual elegance, others freedom and an element of tragedy, yet others a carefree quality and joie de vivre, but in each case it was what she as an artist or fellow human being saw as the essence of the actor. But interestingly, when Mrozovskaya photographed actors in roles, she reverted to the classical St Petersburg model. Here we have no skilfully designed background, no furniture, no other props. The actor is portrayed in an enclosed space, demonstrating the character he is playing. It is as though he is alone with himself and has identified completely with his role. At the same time he is invisibly connected to his audience to form an emotional unity. This is the special feature of her art. Mrozovskaya's favorite subject was the great early-twentieth-century actress Komissarshevs-

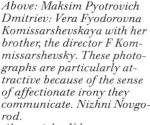

Above: Maksim Pyotrovich Dmitriev: Vera Fyodorovna Komissarshevskaya with her brother, the director F Kommissarshevsky. These photographs are particularly attractive because of the sense of affectionate irony they communicate. Nizhni Novgorod.
Above right: Yelena Mrozovskaya, K A Pasetti: Two photographs of Vera Fyodorovna Komissarshevskaya. The handwriting on the photographs is that of the actress herself.

kaya, and her sets of photographs showing the development of a stage personality are particularly impressive. Some photographs of Komissarshevskaya carry quotations from the play concerned, thus attempting to capture a moment as in performance. Mrozovskaya also photographed Dolina, the singer, and the actor Andreyev-Burlak in the same way.

Officially Mrozovskaya was photographer to "the St Petersburg Conservatory, the Imperial Russian Music Society, at the court of His Royal Highness the Grand Duke of Crna-Gora and the Prince of Bulgaria." She won awards for her work in 1897 in Sweden and in 1900 in France. Her studio was at 20 Nevsky Prospekt, the same place where G K Kirilov did brilliant work in the 1920s, including pictures of Shalyapin and Semenova.

Photographs of actors played a particular role in society life. They were hung on the walls of villas and flats, and used not only to beautify interiors, but also gave information about the artist's taste and sometimes his relationships and contacts. A photograph presented by an actor could mean the beginning of a friendship.

Theatrical photographers expressed intellectual verve, thoughtfulness, joy, and confusion in their work, a lively and touching record of their time. They served art not as a duty, but as a vocation, and thus left us wonderful evidence of our cultural history.

Karl Karlovich Bulla: The
actress Vera Fyodorovna
Kommissarshevskaya.
St Petersburg, c. 1900.

Vera Fyodorovna Komissar-
shevskaya (1864–1910). Famous actress, appeared at
the Alexandrinsky Theater
in St Petersburg from 1896.
She left the state theater in
1902 and founded her own
theater in 1904.

Fyodor Ivanovich Shalyapin
(1873–1938). World-famous
opera singer. Member of the
Moscow Opera 1899–1918.
Successful tours abroad. He
emigrated 1921 and worked
at the Metropolitan Opera
New York from 1921–1925.
He was a gifted actor as well
as the possessor of a unique
bass voice with an enormous
range. His most famous role
was Boris Godunov.

Page 144: M A Scherling, left: Fyodor Ivanovich Shalyapin as Boris Godunov, right above: as Mephistopheles, right below: studioportrait. (All from the Historical Museum, Moscow). Moscow, c. 1900.

Karl Karlovich Bulla, above left: the famous singer Fyodor Ivanovich Shalyapin at his own piano, with Alexander Ivanovich Kuprin, above right: Shalyapin as Boris Godunov, below right: Shalyapin sitting for Ilya Efimovich Repin. (All photographs from the Museum for Theater and Music, Leningrad.) St Petersburg.

M A Scherling, left below: Fedor Ivanovich Chaliapin. (From the Historical Museum, Moscow.) Moscow, c. 1900.

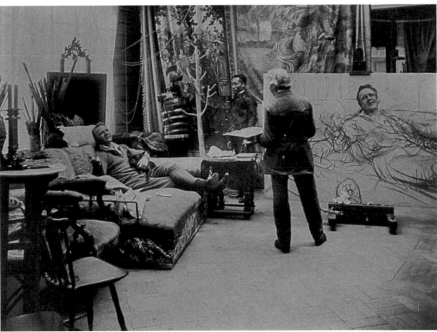

Tatyana Shipova

"A Memory for the Future"*

The archive of the STATE LITERATURE MUSEUM, MOSCOW

*Nikolai A Naidenov

Sergei Lvovich Levitsky: Friedrich Ludwig Jordan, Alexander Andreyevich Ivanov and Pimen Nikitich Orlov, all painters, with a group of friends (daguerreotype). Rome, November 1845.

Photographs are a miracle: they enrich the world, capturing the faces of literati, poets, and artists, and recording past events. Old photos—visiting cards, on mountings stamped in gold or silver on light pink, blue, or black card, printed in shades of violet, blue, sepia, or black. Serried ranks of medals were sometimes shown under the photograph or on the back of the mount.

Typefaces for the mounts were carefully selected, preserving the names and addresses of the firms for us—essential for any photo. Graphic artists' imagination and ingenuity knew no bounds. A world with its own language and symbols grew up, not intended simply for the pursuit of beauty, but subject to its own distinctive rules.

In the 1840s people were fascinated with the new invention, and loved having their photographs taken. It took less time than sitting for a painter, and it was cheaper. In Moscow the principal subjects were the nobility, merchants, and the bourgeoisie, but doctors, pharmacists, officers, civil servants, and even students had their photographs taken as well.

Photographic studios were founded by graduates of the Moscow arts schools and the St Petersburg ACADEMY OF ARTS. Of course a legal framework was needed for all this. Opening a studio, renting, moving, selling photographs, even closing a studio were all under the control of "His Imperial Majesty"—as of 20 March 1858, Section 117. This is an extract from the relevant paragraph: "Permission to open a photographic studio will be granted when the reliability of those persons applying to open the said studio is guaranteed. Application must be made to the Police Chief for the appropriate certificate of reliability."

Fair of 1862: they were not in the section devoted to architecture, art, and painting, but in the section for 'craft tools with a scientific application.'

On 17 October 1862 Assessor Sakharov, the official at the board of censorship responsible for typography and lithography, went into a bookshop. There were photographs on sale, including some pornographic items. He confiscated thirty-four photographs, including a pack of playing cards. Sakharov submitted a report to the chief of police on the same day, and two days later the police made a recommendation to the governor general: "The number of photographs not subject to any legal supervision is increasing annually in Moscow. Thus shops can make these immoral pictures available to the public without incurring any punishment. Do you think it would be possible, on the basis of the above facts, to introduce a series of regulations, especially as far as the above-mentioned photographs are concerned?" From then on all photographic shops and their products were closely observed by the censor's unsleeping eye. The new Press Act of 6 April 1865 affected all traders dealing with photography: "The Chief of Police must make known to all owners of photographic studios that they are forbidden to publish photographs unless they carry the name of the firm. Prints may be produced only by permission of the Board of Censorship."

Albums were originally intended to make it easier to supervise studios. They were used to store all pictures, down to the smallest commission. This was extremely useful in tracing people who lived in Moscow, and the notion seemed so fascinating that the Moscow Police Board's printing department had established a photographic section by 1867. However, this 'photographic documentation' seemed to be not so much in the interests of the police, but more to make available a good pictorial cross-section of the people of Moscow.

If the law was infringed the owner of the studio

Above: Sergei Lvovich Levitsky: Lev Nikolayevich Tolstoy: St Petersburg, 15 February 1856.

Below: Sergei Lvovich Levitsky: Portrait of the author Alexander Vasilyevich Drushinin. St Petersburg, 15 February 1856.

Left: Anonymous: Maria Nikolayevna Tolstaya (daguerreotype). 1845/46.

On receipt of the certificate the aspiring studio owner had to familiarize himself with the relevant statutes and regulations "in order that the studio shall be a fitting part of its district, and readily accessible." There were rigorous fire and smoke regulations, and the owner had to undertake not to pollute any waterway. The business was not allowed to continue once the certificate expired unless and until a new certificate was issued. It was not always possible to acquire a studio precisely where the photographer wished. The Hamburg photographer Eduard Wilhelm Mücke applied to open a studio and was refused for the following reasons: "Mücke intended to install a glass extension in front of two of the windows. This extension would be visible from the belle étage of the governor-general's house. Mücke also intended to put up a wooden shed, which would disfigure one of the most beautiful streets in the town.... For these reasons his request must be refused."

At the time photography was a craft, an occupation. This assessment is confirmed by the place allotted to photographers at the London World

had to pay a fine. The first offense cost twenty silver rubles, the second forty, and the third eighty. If the Police Board's annual reports are to be believed, there were no infringements. There is only one recorded attempt to open a studio without legal permission. Mikhail Ivanov, a farmer, hastily put up a wooden shed with glass windows in his yard, and produced photographs with gay abandon until he was spotted by the watchful eye of the law. All his photographic equipment was confiscated and the shed pulled down. A hearing established that Ivanov had been wandering around the country with his photographic equipment; he had just come from St Petersburg, where he had taken some pictures, then came to Moscow and worked for only a short time—but his preference was for working in the provinces, and he never stayed anywhere for any length of time. The governor was lenient: he ordered all Ivanov's photographic equipment to be returned, but only on condition that he did not use it for money-making purposes.

Photography developed like lightning in all possible directions: technical equipment was improved, studios changed, trade in reagents rapidly increased. Lithographers acccepted numerous commissions for visiting cards. Photographers compared notes in the pages of the new specialized magazines.

In Russia in the 1850s and 1860s the Daguerre process existed alongside photographs printed from negatives. Miniature daguerreotype portraits were not unlike painted miniatures in design. They were delivered in leather cases with attractive clasps, and designed in such a way that they could be worn as pendants. There is a daguerreotype of this kind of Tolstoy's sister Maria Nikolayevna taken in about 1845, when she was fifteen years old. Unfortunately the identity of the photographer is not known.

There were manufacturers specializing in cases, wallets, and frames for daguerreotypes. Barash had a workshop in Bolshaya Dmitrovka Street in Moscow, and a second one by the Kazansky Bridge in St Petersburg.

A G Blumenthal was from Berlin. His studio, Daguerreotypes and Miniature Portraits, was in Gasetnyi Alley opposite an information office. Nistrem wrote: "Blumenthal's daguerreotype studio has existed for some time, but it has now been refurbished and its technical facilities improved. The portraits are perfect likenesses and beautifully finished. Sittings can be arranged every day between ten in the morning and one in the afternoon—in any weather. There is a scale of charges from three silver rubles to ten silver rubles, depending on the nature of the work. If the customer wishes, the miniature portraits can be transferred to ivory by a special daguerreotype process; such portraits are particularly striking. Long, tiring sessions of the kind needed by portrait painters are not needed for this process."

In the 1860s Blumenthal had a studio in Ligovka Street in St Petersburg, then in later years opened another studio in Kutsnietshny Alley near St Vladimir's.

Moscow daguerreotypists sought out the liveliest streets in town for their studios and shops, as near the big department stores as possible. Shopping centers of this kind were to be found in Petrovka Street, Tverska Street and above all by Kuznietsky Bridge, where a shopping arcade had been built in the form of a glass gallery. It was later owned by a businessman called Solodovnikov. In 1840 Prince Golitsyn built a shopping gallery by the Bolshoi Theater, just by this arcade. The glass roof of the gallery guaranteed good light at all times, and attracted a large number of customers as an architectural phenomenon. This gave Blumenthal the idea of making his studio part of the gallery.

Famous people using Blumenthal's daguerreotype gallery included mathematician Pafnuti Levovich Chebyshev and Tolstoy's sister Maria Nikolayevna. Their portraits dated from the 1850s.

From 1860 A Radietsky, a rich patron, "had expended some energy in perfecting the art of photography in all possible directions. He invites people to contact him—not just experts in photography, but also chemists, physicists, other scientists and artists such as painters. People wishing to learn the arts of photography are welcome to talk to Mr Radietsky," wrote the *Moscow Address Book* in 1860.

The photographic collection in the LITERATURE MUSEUM consists of photographs of writers, poets, and their relations and friends, theatrical photographs, and views of the town. The collection is rightly named *Photographic Encyclopaedia of Writers*, but also gives a marvelous view of the history of photography. One could almost suggest that Russian photography began with a portrait of a group of painters taken by Levitsky. Portraits of this kind were rare for daguerreotypists. This is how the picture came to be taken: on a trip to Italy in early November 1845, Levitsky visited a colony of Russian painters in Rome. Here he met A A Ivanov, who was later to paint the famous *Christ Appears Before the People*, and other painters including Jordan, Pimen and, Orlov. Gogol was also in Italy at the time. The Russian minister of education came to Rome on a visit, and the painters decided to present him with a daguerreotype of the group, an unusual gift. "My first attempt astonished all the painters," Levitsky remembered. Later he also produced a detailed description of the preparation of the plates and specifications of exposures. The daguerreotype itself has unfortunately not survived, but we can form an impression of it from a reproduction in the magazine *Old and New Russia* in December 1879. Levitsky made the decision to become a professional photographer because of his close connection with the world of painting, his friendship with Daguerre himself, and with Dumas the chemist, and his own knowledge of physics and chemistry.

Eleven years later, on 15 February 1856, a group

of young writers for the magazine *Contemporary* posed for Levitsky's lens, now somewhat more modern, in his studio on Nevsky Prospekt. Alexander Vasilyevich Drushinin, critic, writer, and founder of the RUSSIAN LITERARY ARCHIVE, tells us how the portraits were taken: "In the early morning I, *Grigorevich, Turgenev, Tolstoy, Ostrovsky, and *Goncharov met at Levitsky's. Kovalevsky was there already. Our faces were photographed. Our morning in the glass-roofed photographic pavilion was interesting in itself. We looked at the portraits of ourselves and the others, laughed, were generally frivolous and wasted time. The group as such could not be photographed like this, but it worked out successfully in the end."

It was pure chance that Nekrasov, the editor of the magazine, was not present. On 18 February the writers were given their portraits and on the same day, after they had signed their pictures, they presented them to Grigorevich, as the group of friends was leaving St Petersburg, and they were all grateful to Grigorevich for the consistently warm welcome he had extended to

S S Isaakovich: The Chekhov family, standing from left to right: Ivan, Anton, Nikolai, Alexander, M G Chekhov, seated Mikhail, Maria, P E Chekhov, E Y Chekhov, L P Chekhova, and Georgy Chekhov. Taganrog, 1874.

them all. He had been particularly sympathetic to Tolstoy and Kovalevsky, who had arrived from Sebastapol late in 1855.

Grigorevich always kept these oval portraits signed by his colleagues at his side. After his death he left them to his family. In 1940 Yekaterina Alexandrovna Tsurikova left them to the LITERATURE MUSEUM.

A significant part of the photographic collection is made up of family photographs of writers handed over to the musem by relations, including family archives from *Blok, *Dostoyevsky, Korolenko, *Mamim-Sibiryak, Tolstoy, Turgenev, *Chekhov, *Ertel, and others.

Daguerreotypes and photographs were collected in Russian archives from a very early stage, shortly after they first began to appear. Various documents report this, among them Drushinin's diary, in which he recorded the portraits he intended to order next. This was quite a long list: "Portraits: don't forget the collection including Miss Mary, Brother Andrei Fedotov, Shdanovich, Lisa, LA. And the others: Satin, Kamensky, Markevich, Drenteln, Svoev, Tolstoy, brother with wife and children, the Shukovskis. ..." He ordered these portraits from Levitsky, whom he knew slightly. "This morning I went over to Levitsky's to collect the portraits, but they had not come out. They will have to be taken again." This entry is dated 14 February 1854.

Early photographic portraits were usually retouched and finished off with water colors. Tulinov and Kramskoy, photographers from Moscow, wrote about this in their memoirs. Drushinin's diary entry about costs for the last few months makes quite amusing reading, especially the notes about "sundry expenditures", which included the daguerreotypes: "We are trying to remember where all the money went. Daguerreotypes, 7; lunch, 10; entertainment, 15; presents, 10; wine, 10; books and theater, 10. That all seems to have slipped through our fingers, and there is simply no sign

of the hundred rubles." This amazement was expressed on 19 December 1853. It is clear from his diary that Levitsky took pictures of the writers from the magazine *Contemporary* again in early March. On 6 March many of them exchanged portraits, many of them again signed: "From A Drushinin to Botkin, 6 March 1856." Unfortunately Drushinin's collection has not survived. There is only one picture in the LITERATURE MUSEUM, showing his mother's country estate in the village of Marinskoye.

In the 1870s the technical processes were simplified, and this led to considerable expansion, particularly in the amateur field. Whole series of family portraits and pictures of the immediate vicinity were taken, and people became more interested in collecting photographs. Many writers now started to take photographs themselves, like Lev Tolstoy, for example, who produced a self-portrait, and Vladimir Galaktionovich Korolenko stopped making pencil sketches and went over to the camera.

Chekhov was another writer who included photography among his skills, and in fact the LITERATURE MUSEUM's most wide-ranging collection comes from his private archive—a valuable source for us, rich in detail. Chekhov frequently received portraits from colleagues, painters, and actors. Many of his friends were capable photographers themselves, and took photographs of the great writer. Thanks to Chekhov's sister Maria Pavlovna, who was particularly fond of portraits, many unique pictures of him have survived—from the earliest picture (1874) to the last photograph, which shows Chekhov shortly before his death. The part of the collection showing Sakhalin island, to which prisoners were banished, is particularly important, as there are understandably few photographs of the place. Equally important are portraits of friends in Melichovo and Yalta.

A writer's private collection of photographs is useful to him not just as a memento, but also as

Anonymous: The first troup of actors at the Moscow Arts Theater with their autographs. Moscow, 1900.

working material; the Sakhalin collection, for example, shows the route he took. Chekhov started to take an interest in the subject of Sakhalin when he was thirty. He worked through all the literature he was able to find about the place on the nature of the trials held and the history of arrests and banishments in Russia, and also on the history of colonization on the island. His sister and her friends helped him by visiting the RUMYANTSOV LIBRARY and transcribing extracts from rare books.

On 21 April 1890 Chekhov traveled from the Yaroslavl Station in Moscow to Sakhalin, with a *New Times (Novoye Vrema)* press pass in his pocket. Members of his family and friends came to see him off. There is a photograph of the group outside the house in Sadovo-Kudrinskaya Street—taken by his younger brother Mikhail, his niece Yevgeniya tells us.

It was not an easy journey: Chekhov did not reach Sakhalin until 11 June, and it was 30 June before the commandant of the island gave him permission to make statistical investigations, examine prison buildings and facilities, talk to banished persons and prisoners doing forced labor, and visit the settlements.

In the northern part of the island of Sakhalin, Chekhov visited mines, camps and prisons such as Duiskaya and Voyevodskaya: "Prisoners convicted of serious crimes are held in the cells in Duiskaya, most of them repeate offenders and prisoners on remand. . . . In Voyevodskaya, some prisoners are chained to wheelbarrows." Chekhov worked in the southern part of Sakhalin from 11 September to 13 October 1890.

"Sakhalin is a place of the most extreme and intolerable suffering of which a human being is capable, whether he is free or a prisoner. . . . I

have discovered from books and other sources that we caused millions of human beings to rot in the prisons, without thinking about it at all, barbarically. . . . No, I assure you, Sakhalin is necessary, and interesting, and one can only regret that I am the person traveling to it, and not someone who knows more about the situation, who would be able to arouse society's interest in it." This is from a letter to Suvorin, editor of the *New Times* on 19 March 1890.

On 11 September he summed up: "I lived in the north of Sakhalin for exactly two months, and did a lot of work, enough material for three diplomas. In other words, there is not a single forced laborer or settler I haven't spoken to. I was particularly successful in counting up the children, a task which seemed especially important to me."

Chekhov traveled home by sea, after being given a passport in Vladivostok. His route took him along the coast of Asia, across the Indian Ocean, and through the Suez Canal in order to reach Odessa via Constantinople. The journey also

took him to Ceylon, where he used the railway for a winter journey. Here he bought two mongooses, which he took back to Moscow. In May 1895 the volume *Sakhalin Island* was published by the *Russian Thought (Russkaya Miysl)* press.

Chekhov valued the photographs of Tolstoy taken by Tolstoy's wife particularly highly. Sofia Andreyevna started to take photographs in 1887, and learned about technical processes from the beginning. She kept up the hobby for twenty years, and took pictures of Tolstoy, the children, relations and friends. She was generous in giving them to friends and relations as well.

Chekhov and Tolstoy knew each other from 1895. Chekhov visited Yasnaya Polyana on 8 and 9 August of that year. "I spent one and a half days in his home. The impressions are wonderful. I felt completely at home, and Tolstoy was easy to talk to. I will tell you more when we meet," he wrote to Suvorin. While he was there, Chertkov and Gorbunov were reading Tolstoy's novel *Re-*

I I Pavlovsky: The village of the exiles. (From Chekhov's private collection.) Sakhalin.

*I I Pavlovsky: Prisoners are
chained before work in Duiskaya jail. (From Chekhov's
private collection.) Sakhalin.*

I I Pavlovsky: Prisoners at work. (From Chekhov's private collection.) Sakhalin.

Above: Pyotr Alexeyevich Sergeyenko: Tolstoy and Chekhov at the Panina dacha, below: retouched version. 12 September 1901.

Right: Sofia Andreyevna Tolstaya: Chekhov and Tolstoy in Gaspra. 12 September 1901.

surrection. After Chekhov had given his opinion of the novel he pointed put an inaccuracy in the sentencing of Katyusha Maslova. As he had studied legal procedure so carefully, he knew that none could be condemned to forced labor for as short a time as Tolstoy's original manuscript suggested. The great man corrected the mistake.

The two writers' second meeting took place in Tolstoy's house in Moscow. Chekhov was given an portrait of Tolstoy, signed "To Chekhov from Tolstoy, 14 February 1896." Chekhov noted in his diary: "I called on Tolstoy as I was passing through Moscow. He was on edge, spoke hurriedly about decadents, and quarreled with Chitsherin for an hour and a half. Chitsherin seemed to me to be talking nothing but nonsense the whole time."

The two writers did not become really close until the time in 1901 when they lived only a few miles away from each other in the Crimea, Chekhov in Autka, Tolstoy on Gaspra, in Panina's house. The two writers met frequently. Photographs were taken on one of these occasions by the writer Sergeyenko and Sofia Andreyevna. Sergeyenko took a group photograph on the balcony of the house on 12 September

1901. On one photograph everyone except Chekhov and Tolstoy was retouched out of the picture, and signs of this retouching can clearly be seen on the negative. Kuprin remembered this photograph: "In my house in Gatshino I have a photograph of Tolstoy and Chekhov. ... Tolstoy was so deep in conversation that he forgot about his breakfast. He held his spoon in such a way, with his fingers very near the end, that it looked as though he was threatening Chekhov. Chekhov was smiling pleasantly, but somewhat archly (incidentally, I have never seen a smile more beautiful than Chekhov's). It looked as though Tolstoy was saying to Chekhov: 'Firstly, Anton Pavlovich, one should write much more simply!' and Chekhov's shy smile replied: 'Lev Nikolaiyevich, that is the most difficult thing in the world.'" The photograph is kept in a simple wooden frame of just the kind that Chekhov used.

Chekhov's collection also contains part of the photographic legacy of Maria Pavlovna Chekhova, a teacher and painter, who founded the Chekhov Museum in Yalta. Her photos make it clear that after the writer's death in 1904 his friends continued to visit the house, and never forgot his mother and sister. The collection includes a fine portrait of the young Bunin with the inscription: "To the charming, magnificent, beautiful Maria Pavlovna from Bukishon."

There are also some portraits by Shipkina-Kupernik, who had been a family friend throughout her life. She was a poet, and a very fine translator of Rostand, Shakespeare, and Molière. One of the portraits she inscribed with a winter poem, in which she described Maria Pavlovna as "calendar of my life":

Leonid Valentinovich Sredin: Anton Pavlovich Chekhov and Maksim Gorky. Yalta, 5 May 1900.

Calendar of my life
Together we met the spring
The summer days are gone
Then came the autumn—summer for old women
May we wait long for the winter

to the faithful M P Chekhova
from her faithful friend
January 1912, T Shepkina-Kupernik

Above: Yelena Mrozovskaya: N A Podgorny of the Moscow Arts Theater in the role of Fedotik in "Three Sisters". St Petersburg, 1901.

Right: F Opitz: Scenes from "Uncle Vanya" and "Three Sisters". (Moscow Arts Theater.) Moscow, 1899–1901.

In 1898 Konstantin Stanislavsky and Vladimir Nemirovich Dantshenko founded the Moscow ARTS THEATER. Chekhov's artistic association with this theater was mutually enriching. The young dramatist's ideas chimed with the new theater's search for new expressive possibilities. The production of *The Seagull* in 1898 was a theatrical breakthrough, and the performances were an absolute triumph. After one of them the audience sent Chekhov a greeting signed by over three hundred people. On 1 May 1899 the actors gave a special performance for the dramatist, who had come to Moscow. On 7 May of the same year Chekhov had his photograph taken with the cast of *The Seagull*. The dramatist's bond with the theater was made even tighter by *Uncle Vanya*. Chekhov was present in person at the rehearsals. The theater also put on plays by Gerhard Hauptmann and

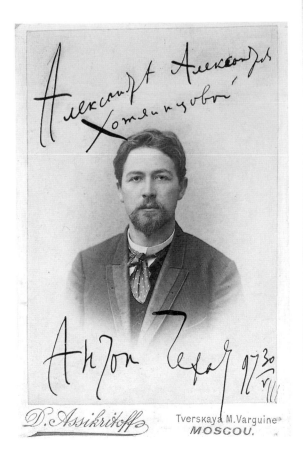

P P Pavlov: Chekhov with actors from the Moscow Arts Theater. Moscow, 7 May 1899.

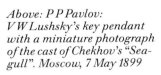

Above: P P Pavlov: V W Lushsky's key pendant with a miniature photograph of the cast of Chekhov's "Seagull". Moscow, 7 May 1899

Left: D Asikritov: Chekhov, with dedications in his own hand. Moscow, 1893.

Henrik Ibsen. In November 1900 Chekhov was invited to the premiere of Ibsen's *When We Dead Awaken*. The actors made wicked use of this title, and presented Chekhov with a portrait of the full company bearing the inscription: "When will we dead awaken? When Anton Pavlovich writes a new play for us!" They wrote witty remarks round the edges of the photograph, and appended their signatures. Chekhov's collection of theatrical photographs is rounded off with pictures of productions of *Uncle Vanya* and *Three Sisters*. The premiere of *The Cherry Orchard* on 17 January 1904 coincided with the playwright's birthday and the twenty-fifth anniversary of his career as a writer. Few people knew that a celebration had been planned—even Chekhov himself had no idea about it. His appearance on the stage was greeted with thunderous applause. Speeches were made by the SOCIETY OF FRIENDS OF RUSSIAN LITERATURE and also by the publishers of the magazines *Russian Thought* and *Children Reading*. The actress G N Fedotova represented

the Maly Theater: "The Maly Theater has not had the good fortune of welcoming a beloved writer who has written a new and beautiful page in the great book of Russian literature, but the sincerity and force of our greeting is made neither smaller nor weaker by this." Two actors from the MOSCOW ARTS THEATER, Lushsky and Samarova, presented Chekhov with an antique case containing portraits of all the theater's actors and students. Most of the portraits from this collection are now in the LITERATURE MUSEUM. They were taken by Albert Ivanovich Mei, one of the best photographers in Moscow. Some wonderful views of old Moscow taken by him bring this chapter to a close.

Below: Leonid Valentinovich Sredin: Anton Pavlovich Chekhov in his study. Yalta, 1901.

Right: Aleksei P Chekhov: Anton Pavlovich Chekhov, 1897

Albert Ivanovich Mey:
Cathedral of Christ the
Redeemer. Moscow,
1880–1890.

Page 162/163: Albert Ivano-
vich Mey: Street scene. From
the album Views of Moscow.
Moscow, 1880–1890.

Albert Ivanovich Mey: View
from the Ivan the Great bell
tower in the Kremlin. From
Views of Moscow. *Moscow,*
1880–1890.

Albert Ivanovich Mey: View from the Ivan the Great bell tower in the Kremlin. From Views of Moscow. *Moscow, 1884.*

Albert Ivanovich Mey:
Ochotnije-lane. (Ochotnije
means hunter). A former
market place, where hunters
sold furs. 1888.

*Anonymous: View of Novaya
Basmanaya Street. From*
Views of Moscow. *Moscow,
1880–1890.*

Otto Kirchner: Sucharevs-
kaya Square. Moscow,
1 September 1902.

*Otto Kirchner: Lynbyans-
kaya Square. Moscow,
12 September 1902.*

Alexandra Golovina

Preserved for Posterity

The collection of the STATE CENTRAL ARCHIVE
OF FILM AND PHOTOGRAPHIC DOCUMENTARY, Leningrad

This collection has an interesting history. On 4 February 1926 the COUNCIL OF PEOPLE'S COMMISSARS OF THE RUSSIAN SOCIALIST FEDERATIVE SOVIET REPUBLICS issued a decree *Concerning the handing over of negatives, photographs and film which are of interest in the context of Revolution*. A photographic section of the LENINGRAD REGIONAL PICTURE LIBRARY was founded in August 1936, and in 1941 it became part of the STATE ARCHIVE FOR DOCUMENTS OF THE OCTOBER REVOLUTION AND THE ESTABLISHMENT OF SOCIALISM. In 1966 the archive became independent, as the LENINGRAD STATE ARCHIVE OF FILM AND PHOTOGRAPHIC DOCUMENTARY. It had its present name since 1987.

It holds almost half a million documentary photographs dating from 1860 to 1917. A major part of the collection consists of original negatives, some of which are rare, if not unique. Every year there is an enormous influx of new photographs from municipal authorities, from organizations and firms, and from private and family collections.

The archive also contains photographs from the period before and after the October Revolution, and I should like to concentrate on this period in the present chapter. We owe the most detailed pictorial documentation of the events of 1917 in

Petrograd to a photo-reporter called Steinberg. His photographs of the period are a visual diary of the eventful days of the Revolution, showing major episodes in Petrograd—the committal of the victims of the 1917 February Revolution, demonstrations on the Champ de Mars, the

Anonymous: Wandering beggars in a small, unidentified provincial town. 1889.

Anonymous: Peasants from
the St Petersburg area.
C. 1900.

Unidentifiable photo of a typically Russian scene. St Petersburg, c. 1900.

Red Guards at a campfire in the streets of Petrograd.

Pavel Semenovich Shukov (1870–1942) is an important figure among the photographers who documented the revolution. The archive holds about fifteen hundred negatives left by Shukov, taken between 1902 and 1936. He came to St Petersburg after finishing at secondary school and started his apprenticeship with C Shapiro, a famous St Petersburg photographer of his time. Shukov learned numerous aspects of photography from 1902 to 1917 in Shapiro's studio at 18 Nevsky Prospekt, but most of his work in this period consisted of portraits of important scientists, artists, and literati.

Photographs by the well-known St Petersburg photographer Karl Karlovich Bulla and his sons Alexander and Victor are among the most numerous in the collection—almost a hundred thousand negatives.

K K Bulla (1855–1930) was one of the first photojournalists in Russia. In 1875 he set up his photographic studio at 61 Sadovaya Street and mainly took portraits for the next ten years. From 1886, when he received his craftsman's certificate conferring "the right to photograph views in the metroplis and its surroundings," Bulla concerned himself with pictorial reporting and soon became photographic correspondent for a number of Russian and foreign magazines.

From 1886 Bulla's studio was at 110 Nevsky Prospekt. His ability to satisfy his exclusive clientele's requirements, his smooth, rapid completion of work ordered, and above all his astonishing capacity for hard work gained him the reputation of being one of the best photographers in St Petersburg.

In 1896 Bulla acquired the title of "Photographer to the Ministry of the Imperial Court". This title gave Bulla better opportunities to find the best spot for his camera on special occasions. He was given a certificate allowing him to take "photographs of military maneuvers, troop

smashing of the offices of the Petrograd Committee of the RSDAP(B) in the Villa Krzesinska. On 8 July 1917 Steinberg took a picture of the disarming of the First Regiment of Machine Gunners, who had taken an active part on the workers' side in the 1917 July Demonstration. On 27 October 1917 he photographed a passport check on the way into Smolny and in the very first days of the October Revolution a patrol of

*Anonymous: Blind beggars
taking a rest. 1900.*

Anonymous: Floods on the River Neva, seen from the University quay. St Petersburg was prone to frequent flooding; not until after the Revolution were dams built outside the town to contain the floods. St Petersburg, 1903.

inspections, military drills, launching, and ships at anchor in the territory of the St Petersburg military guard."

During the last ten years in which he practiced (1904–1914), Bulla produced a tremendous number of pictures on military subjects, showing the life of military staff, and troops in great detail. The photographs capture military drill and sporting competitions, parades, maneuvers, troop inspections, interiors of barracks, canteens, and mess rooms, and large numbers of individual and group portraits of soldiers, officers, and generals.

The strike in the Putilov factory triggered the outbreak of the revolution of 1905. Bulla took some historic pictures at the time, showing striking workers at the factory gate and in the streets of St Petersburg on the evening before the famous procession to the Winter Palace. One of his series of pictures makes it clear that the imperial government had a vicious bloodbath prepared to greet the peaceful demonstration: army and police units had been concentrated at the Narva Gate, in the Palace Square, and in all the streets through which the demonstration was due to pass.

These pictures are an important source of historical information, reflecting the level of development of industry, trade, and the municipal and rural infrastructure. This material is particularly valuable because Russian archives hold very few photographs showing economic development before the October Revolution.

It was not until the late nineteenth century that pictorial reporters began to turn their attention to industrial subjects, and K K Bulla was an early

Anonymous: View of the Fontanka River between the Anishkov and Semenovsky bridges. This photo shows why St Petersburg was called the Venice of the North. St. Petersburg, c. 1900.

and successful pioneer. He visited factories, production co-operatives, and small workshops. Here he photographed production processes, firms' products, factory and workshop interiors, and the everyday lives of workers and officials. Our archive also holds striking pictures of the building and launching of warships. Bulla produced negatives of almost every ship in the imperial fleet. Pictures showing the building of the ironclads *Borodino, Orjol*, and *Poltova* and the battleship *Gangut* in the Admiralty yards are of particular documentary interest.

In the early years of this century, a firm called Russian Renault became Russia's largest car producer. Bulla prepared a series on cars, factory interiors of car factories, and individual production sites, and he photographed the workers themselves on assembly lines or manufacturing parts. The aircraft industry was captured on film in factories in St Petersburg and Riga, and thorough coverage of the electrotechnical industry was also provided in pictures showing the building of radio stations, the installation of radio equipment, and the early telephones and electrotechnical controls and measuring devices.

Fires and floods were the most terrible natural catastrophes faced by the inhabitants of St Petersburg. Bulla also worked as official photographer to the ASSOCIATION OF RUSSIAN FIRE BRIGADES, and every major fire of the period was recorded by him. All three members of the Bulla family took pictures of floods.

Bulla was also official photographer to many institutions of higher education in St Peters-

Anonymous: Unloading a barge. One of the rare photographs showing workers in action. It would seem that even the photographers who called themselves democratic could get little out of this subject. St Petersburg, 1900.

Anonymous: The Admiralty quay seen from Vasievsky Island. This pictures shows vividly what a lively trading center the city was, further emphasized by the many different kinds of ship. St Petersburg, 1912/13.

Page 178/179: Anonymous: Yachts and motor boats on the Fontanka at Kalinkin Bridge quay. A tram can be seen in the background. The unknown photographer had an excellent eye for perspective and the formal possibilities of the medium. St Petersburg, 1913.

Page 180/181: Anonymous: Weekly market on Nevsky Prospekt, outside the Gostiny Dvor department store. St Petersburg, 1900.

burg, and official photographer to the PUBLIC LIBRARY. He took photographs of practically all the most important academic symposia and conferences, and provided portraits of academy members, well-known scholars and assistants in academic institutions, professors, and lecturers, as well as students at lectures and in laboratories.

The Bulla family also provided important material on the life of Leo Tolstoy on his estate at Yasnaya Polyana. In July 1908, immediately before the celebrations for Tolstoy's eightieth birthday, K K Bulla and his son Victor visited him at Yasnaya Polyana. More than ninety photographs were taken, including Tolstoy, his close relations, everyday family life, the interior of the house, views of Yasnaya Polyana and its environs.

Photographers from the Bulla family were frequent visitors to the suburb of St Petersburg known as Penaty. The famous Russian painter Ilya Repin lived and worked here. There is a great deal of visual material on Repin and his

family, including photocopies of his paintings. The surviving photos show famous Russian artists and other cultural figures: V V Andreyev, F I Shalyapin, *Glazunov, *Pavlova, Blok, and Gorky.

K K Bulla's professional activity ended after he left Petrograd in 1916 and settled on Esel Island, where he spent the last years of his life.

Alexander Karlovich Bulla (1881–1943) trained as a photographer in Germany. After returning to Russia in 1909 he became his father's assistant and specialized in studio photography. Alexander Bulla made a name as a portrait photographer, but did not restrict himself entirely to studio work. He was also involved in his father's pictorial reportage. He first published photo essays of his own in the magazine *Russian Sun* and after victory in the October Revolution in the magazine *The Flame*.

The period 1922 to 1927 was one of the most productive in Alexander Bulla's creative development as a pictorial reporter, and many press photographs bore the signature A Bulla. He sometimes worked with his younger brother Viktor, and the photographs were then signed 'Bulla Brothers'. Viktor Karlovich Bulla (1883–1938) saw himself as a pictorial reporter from an early stage. After completing his studies at the English Institute in St Petersburg (1899) he worked on a number of assignments with his father and elder brother.

Viktor Bulla produced his first independent pictorial photo essays from the battlefields of the Russo-Japanese war (1904–5). His camera captured fighting in exposed positions close to the front. He showed such disregard for personal danger that he was awarded a medal for bravery for his commitment and courage on the Domensky Pass.

All three of the Bulla family of photographers worked at the front in three wars—the Russo-Japanese, the First World War, and the Russian Civil War. From the early days of the First World War, both Alexander and Viktor Bulla

Anonymous: The famous Bulla photographic dynasty: standing in the middle is Karl K Bulla, to his left Alexander K Bulla and on the right Victor K Bulla. St Petersburg, 1914/15.

Karl Karlovich Bulla: Demonstration on 1 May during the first Russian Revolution, organized by Bolsheviks from St Petersburg and Finnish revolutionaries. Terijoki, Finland, 1906.

Victor Karlovich Bulla: Lev Nikolayevich Tolstoy and Karl Karlovich Bulla on the veranda of Tolstoy's house. Bulla and his son Victor had traveled to Yasnaya Polyana on the occasion of the writer's eightieth birthday, and took about ninety photographs of Tolstoy and his family. July 1908.

Page 185: Anonymous: Tolstoy with his daughter Alexandra. The picture was taken directly in front of the veranda of Tolstoy's house and was probably by Karl Bulla. Yasnaya Polyana, July 1908 (?).

photographed important engagements and operations at the front, and their father provided newspapers and magazines with important information from Petrograd. These include the Nevsky Prospekt in the early days of the war; group portraits of officers and soldiers before their departure for the front; street demonstrations and student protests; pictures of Tsar Nicholas II reading the declaration of war from the balcony of the Winter Palace; pictures of the general mobilization; nurses in training.

The archive also holds a full range of material on political life in Petrograd immediately before the Revolution. Thousands of people went on to the streets to protest against the shooting of workers on the Lena goldfields (north-east Siberia) in April 1912. The urban proletariat began to strike. Victor Bulla took a series covering such mass scenes and demonstrations.

The strike movement grew steadily, and in February 1917 led to open mass demonstrations against the Tsarist autocracy. On 23 February (8 March) 1917 Victor Bulla photographed a massive demonstration by women who had taken to the streets carrying red banners and shouting "Down with the Tsar! Down with war! Give us bread!"

Barricades went up in the streets. Workers in revolt smashed police stations, broke open prisons, tore down Tsarist emblems and coats of arms, and arrested policemen. Troops of red guards were formed in factories and major firms. Viktor Bulla was there as an eyewitness of these historic events, and his camera captured the revolutionary rising of the proletariat of Petrograd on film. The captions speak for themselves: "Tearing down the imperial arms from the tower of the Army and Navy Build-

Above: Anonymous: Opening of the summer season in Catherine's Court. Workers' families have made themselves comfortable on the grass. St Petersburg, 1911.

Right: Anonymous: Participant in the world wrestling championships. St Petersburg, 1912.

new heights. Spontaneous demonstrations broke out in Petrograd. Troops loyal to the government began to occupy the principal streets and squares. Viktor Bulla photographed a group of workers making machine-gun belts in an arms factory. He was also responsible for the world-famous picture of the shooting of peaceful demonstrators on 4 July 1917. He took this from the roof of the Passage building while un-

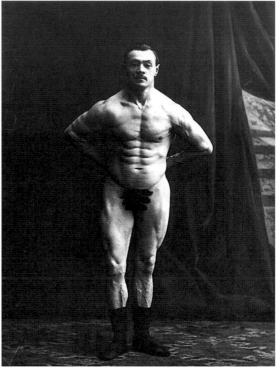

ing," "At the local Palace of Justice on Liteyny Prospekt," "Arrested policemen being escorted into the State Duma Building," "After the smashing of the Police Archive Building," "Fire Department after the major fire," "Burning the Tsar's emblem," "Smashing the Preliminary Interrogation Building," "Barricades at the local Palace of Justice," "Volunteers join the People's Militia in the City Council."

On 18 April (1 May) 1917, a people's holiday was declared and celebrated for the first time in Russia—the day of International Workers' Solidarity. Marching columns of demonstrators with solemn slogans and flags filled the streets and squares of St Petersburg. Spontaneous demonstrations broke out all over the city, speakers addressed the crowds. Viktor Bulla took a series of pictures on the Nevsky Prospekt and by the Alexander Column in the Palace Square.

In late June 1917 the political situation throughout the country became more serious. The universally detested First World War ground on. Factories closed down and unemployment was on the increase. Popular discontent reached

der fire from machine guns and rifles. This rare photograph confirms the tragic fact of deliberate provocation by the Provisional Government, the shooting of defenseless people by Junkers and Cossacks.

This chapter has concentrated largely on events before and after the October Revolution, but the photographs show the range of subjects covered by our archive. We hope these photographs serve to give you an impression of the history and everyday life of St Petersburg–Petrograd–Leningrad.

Anonymous: Festively dressed strollers in the summergardens. St Petersburg, 1911.

Anonymous: Launching the cruiser Aurora. On 25 October 1917 the ship sailed up the Neva to St Petersburg as far as the Winter Palace and there fired its guns as a signal that the palace should be stormed. Today the ship is a floating museum on the Neva. St Petersburg, 1900.

*Anonymous: Konka on
Nevsky Prospekt, outside
number 38. Konkas were
horse-drawn trams that
handled a large proportion of
public transport. St Petersburg, 1908.*

Anonymous: Administrators and workers at the telephone exchange looking at a newly-installed telegraph system. Most such technical equipment was largely imported from France and Germany. St Petersburg, 1907.

Page 196/197: Anonymous: Celebrations for the three-hundredth anniversary of the House of Romanov. This photograph is a good example—even though the photographer's identity is unknown—of what it meant to be appointed court photographer: you were allotted a privileged position from which to take the photograph. St Petersburg, 1913.

Anonymous: Three-hundredth anniversary of the House of Romanov. Tsar Nicholas II and Tsarina Alexandra at the Winter Palace. St Petersburg, 1913.

Anonymous: Three-hundredth anniversary of the House of Romanov. Spectators for the celebrations, held all over the country, came from the most far-flung villages. This anniversary was practically the last demonstration of the splendor and power of the Tsars in Russia. Kostroma, 1913.

*Anonymous: The railway
line crossing Lake Ladoga,
into which the Neva flows.
The line was built in the winter, when the ice was strong
enough to bear it. 1914.*

*Anonymous: In the early
stages of the war: passers-by
read the special edition of*
Evening News (Veshernoe
Vremya). *St Petersburg,
August 1914.*

Above: Anonymous: Demonstration supporting Serbia in its rejection of Austria-Hungary's ultimatum. Because of pressure from Germany it was formulated sharply, and thus unacceptable to Serbia. St Petersburg, 1914.

Below: Anonymous: Mobilization. Reservists go to the barracks accompanied by family and friends. St Petersburg, July 1914.

Page 203: Anonymous. First World War: recruits departing for the front. Petrograd (?), 1916.

*G Fried: This photo shows
how much the First World
War had already changed the
face of war: soldiers of the
Duchovshinsky Regiment
practicing the use of gas
masks. 1916/1917.*

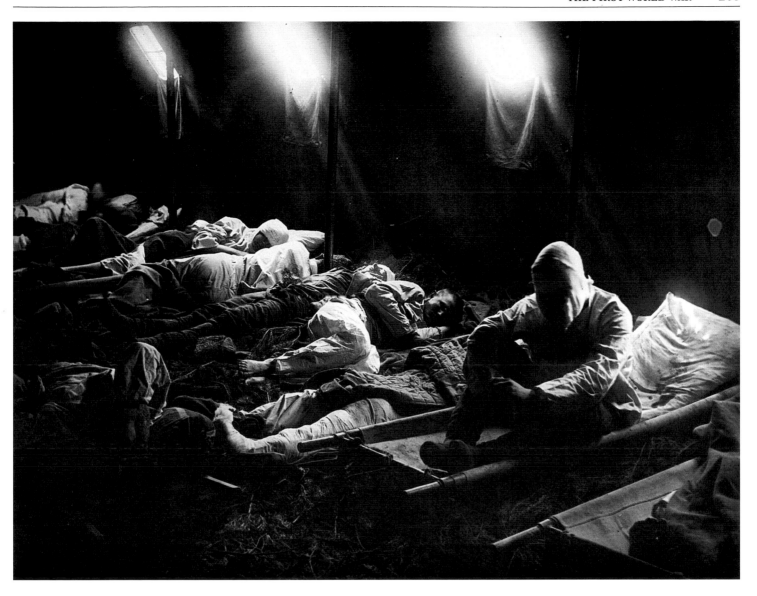

G Fried. First World War: wounded soldiers in the field hospital. 1915–1917.

Anonymous: First World War: burial of the fallen soldiers of the Duchovshinsky Regiment. 1915–1917.

G Fried: First World War: military cemetery near the front. 1915–1917.

G Fried: First World War: a
theatrical performance for
soldiers of the Duchov-
shinsky Regiment. 1915–1917.

*G Fried: First World War:
soldiers at a demonstration.
1915–1917.*

G Fried: First World War:
soldiers at a demonstration.
1917.

Anonymous: Revolt on the battleship Potemkin. *This picture enables us to follow physical change gone through by a photograph which is outstanding for historical reasons. The original from which this lithograph was made was frequently reproduced or printed, with the result that it is possible to make out the (old) halftone dots. The picture looks as though it has been retouched, and is thus it has lost the prime attribute of photography—to show what is really there—and has been reduced to a mere sign or symbol. Constanta (Rumania), 1905.*

Albert G Yuskin

The Unforgettable Shape of Russia

The Central State Archive for Russian Film and Photography, Krasnogorsk

Interest in Russian history is on the increase at the moment, particularly at home. We cannot answer questions of the present without looking back into the past. Historical memories and popular traditions have enriched society intellectually and spiritually.

A persistent theme in late-nineteenth-century Russian photography is that of the Russian people. Karelin, Sergei Lobovikov, K K Bulla, and Dmitriev created a world of unforgettable figures. Their work is imbued with the anxieties, joys and sorrows of their times, ordinary people's experience. But photographers did not always think like this. Early photographers were fascinated by the fact that a moment could be captured, that events could be recorded much more quickly than by a painting. It was not until much later that photographers penetrated the depths of everyday life, and made people's private lives and feelings, the flavor of the present for them, into subjects for genre photography. "Genre is the living present," wrote V V Stasov.

Polyakov's work is a good example of this. He was a little-known photographer who produced an album called *Camp of the 38th Regiment of Dragoons, Vladimirsky, near Moshaisk*. Polyakov took the pictures in the summer of 1885. He photographed everyday scenes of military life, but also soldiers with peasants, children, and local people. His photographs have a lyrical atmosphere and and catch the good humor of these encounters. They convey a sense of deep respect for human beings.

Ordinary people in Russia lived wretchedly through difficult years of drought and of cholera and typhoid epidemics: all the photographs convey this. In 1891 and 1892 drought hit the Volga region, and people were driven mad by hunger and sickness. Postcards were printed and the pictures distributed in other regions, which increased social awareness of the disaster and assisted the organization of aid.

Maksim Pyotrovich Dmitriev was definitely one of the most interesting and colorful 'democratic' photographers in the late-nineteenth-century. He took a very unsparing series showing the Volga famine of 1891 and 1892. The series shows his commitment and makes us feel pity for the victims of inescapable poverty.

Dmitriev was also wellknown for ten years (1894–1903) of work on everything concerned with 'Mother Volga', that ancient and mighty Russian river, from its source in Rybinsk to Astrakhan, where it flows into the Caspian Sea. This series includes architectural studies and

genre pictures, characteristic folk scenes and ethnographic photographs. At the same time, in 1897, Dmitriev started work on his album *Russia in the Past*, in which he immortalized the superstitious lumpenproletariat of the Volga area and many other phenomena of the old days. Dmitriev's pictures are a precise reflection of life in prerevolutionary Russia. Late-nineteenth-century Russian photographers had a high level of technical skill. Besides the well-known photographers there were a large number of unknown camera enthusiasts who were often no worse than their teachers. The best example of this are pictures taken of burlaks (barge-towers) by Vasilev, a photographer from Samara; another example is the series *Everyday Worries*, taken by Hahn of St Petersburg. There is a unique album called *Life in the Trenches, April 1917.* This is a collection of material reporting life on the front shortly after the collapse of the monarchy. Alexander Blok, who fought in the Pinsk Marshes from July 1916, wrote about the period in his book *The Last Days of Imperial Power*:

"Europe has gone mad: the flower of humanity,

Above: Anonymous: manufacturing shops in a weaving mill in the Prochorov factory in the Krasnaya Presnya district. Moscow, 1914.

Above left: Anonymous: political exiles in the coal mines. C. 1904.

Below left: Maksim Pyotrovich Dmitriev: manufacturing shops in the Prochorov factory. Moscow, 1914.

Text continued on page 250

Above left: Anonymous: Nikolayevsky harbor on the Volga. 1913.

Above right: Anonymous: blessing from the Orthodox priest. C. 1904.

Below right: Maksim Pyotrovich Dmitriev: Solovatov's house in the Tatar village of Kadomka in the Sergashevsky district. There was severe famine in the Volga region at the time, and thatch from the roofs was removed and fed to the cattle. Kadomka, 1891/92.

Anonymous: Barge-towers on a tributary of the Volga. Burlaks or barge-towers were a common sight. Ilya Repin dedicated his picture Barge-towers on the Volga *to them. C. 1895.*

*A Vasiliev: Fishing boats on
the Volga. From the album*
Nikolai II's visit to Samara,
1 July 1904.

A Vasiliev: Barge-towers (Burlaks) on the Volga. From the album Nikolai II's visit to Samara, 1 July 1904.

K E Hahn (C H de Hahn & Co): Pilgrims and handicapped people coming to the monastery in the hope of being healed. At the time there was no medical provision for these people. From the album The Imperial Family's visit to the Sorovsky desert. *Serafim-Sorovsky, 1903.*

K E Hahn: Pilgrims on the way to the holy places. From the album The Imperial Family's visit to Sorovsky desert. *Serafim-Sorovsky, 1903.*

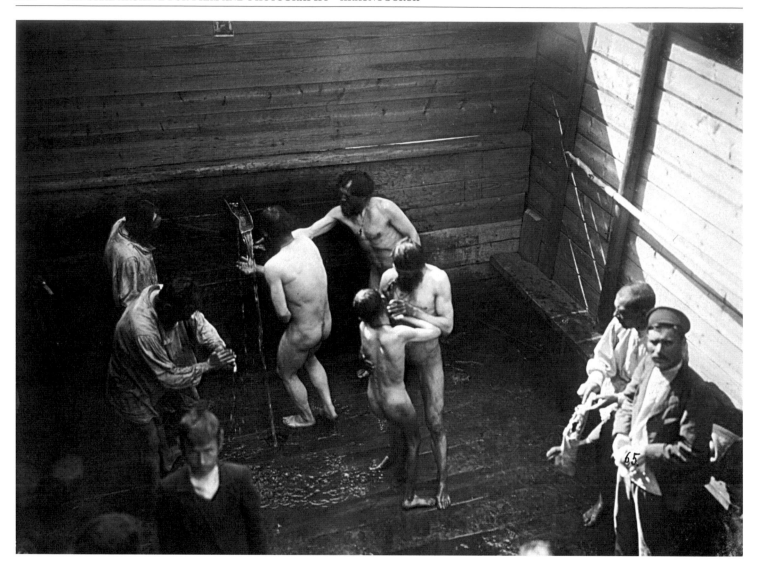

*K E Hahn: At the monas-
tery's sacred spring. People
bathed here, drank the water,
took it away with them.
From the album* The Impe-
rial Family's visit to Sorovsky
desert. *Serafim-Sorovsky,
1903*

K E Hahn: Nikolai II's family at the Sorovsky monastery. From the album The Imperial Family's visit to Sorovsky desert. *Serafim-Sorovsky, 1903.*

K E Hahn: Local clergy with an itinerant monk thought to have Godgiven powers for healing the sick. He came to the monastery on the occasion of the Tsar's visit. From the album The Imperial Family's visit to the Sorovsky desert. *Serafim-Sorovsky, 1903.*

K E Hahn: Women in the local costume of the Volga region waiting for the arrival of the Tsar. From the album The Imperial Family's visit to the Sorovsky desert: *Sera-fim-Sorovsky, 1903.*

K E Hahn: The elders of the
village waiting for the arrival
of the Tsar, to whom they had
been authorized to speak.
They will greet him with a
presentation of bread and
salt. From the album The
Imperial Family's visit to
Sorovsky desert: Serafim-
Sorovsky, 1903.

K E Hahn: Food tents at the monastery. Usually people had to bring their own food (as in this photograph), but on other extraordinary feast days bread and soup were sometimes distributed free. Serafim-Sorovsky, 1903.

K E Hahn: Easter procession. From the album The Imperial Family's visit to the Sorovsky desert. *Tsar Nikolai II had four daughters and he visited many religious sites in the hope of being blessed with a son. Serafim-Sorovsky, 1903.*

Anonymous: Early industrial photograph of copper mines owned by the Syiserskaya factory. From the album Industry in the town of Zlatoust. *The town was known as an industrial center. Slatoust near Samara, 1894.*

*Anonymous: Building the
canal between the St Gleb
and St Elexei locks. Near
St Petersburg, 1905–1910.*

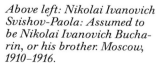

Above left: Nikolai Ivanovich Svishov-Paola: Assumed to be Nikolai Ivanovich Bucharin, or his brother. Moscow, 1910–1916.

Above right: Nikolai Ivanovich Svishov-Paola: Married couple. If this photographer saw interesting faces in the street, he asked them to sit for him, which is probably what happened in this case. Moscow, c. 1902.

Below right: Nikolai Ivanovich Svishov-Paola: Presumably a self-portrait, taken in his studio in Kutsnetsky Most. Moscow, 1910–1920.

Above: Nikolai Ivanovich Svishov-Paola: Well-known patron Savva I Mamontov, an unusual personality in cultural life around the turn of the century. He organized distinguished circles, groups of artists and discussion salons in Moscow and Abramcevo (near Moscow). Moscow, c. 1902.

Left: Nikolai Ivanovich Svishov-Paola: Beggar, typical face of an old Russian of the period. The photographer paid his model a sum of money for sitting for him. Moscow, c. 1902.

Above right: Tsar Alexander III's family. The Tsar is on the right of the picture, at the front on the left his wife Maria Fedorovna, left the eldest son Nikolai, later Tsar Nikolai II. 1891–1894.

Below right: Anonymous: Nikolai II and Kaiser Wilhelm with entourage at the Borgsdorf railway station. 1910.

Below left: Kessler: Tsarevich Nikolai Alexandrovich takes his seat in the carriage. He is being greeted by the crowd. The Tsar's heir makes his acquaintance with the Russian people. Novsherkask, 1891.

*K E Hahn: Before Tsar Niko-
lai II's ceremonial speech on
the day of the opening of the
State Council and the State
Duma. In the Winter Palace,
St Petersburg, 27 April 1906.*

I Kovalsky: Alexander III's family among close friends hunting in Opala. It was his last hunt, as he died in November. He usually hunted in Belovshkaya Pusha. Presumably Belovshkaya Pusha, September 1894.

K E Hahn: Nikolai II and his daughter Olga with officers of the Elizavatgrad regiment of Hussars, of which Olga was Commander-in-Chief. She was a figurehead, rather than a commander on active service. Carskoye Selo, 1910–1915

GRIGORI Y RASPUTIN
(1821–1916)
Rasputin a peasant from the Tobolsk area who gave himself out to be a wandering prophet and mystic, gained considerable influence over Nicholas II, and even more over his wife Alexandra. They believed that he had cured the heir to the throne, Alexei—born after four daughters—of incurable hemophilia. Alexandra in particular was obsessed with the notion that her son's life and with it the fate of the Russian empire depended on Rasputin. The "holy devil" was murdered in 1916 by men hoping to save the monarchy.

Above: Anonymous: Portraits of Grigori Rasputin. St Petersburg, 1910–1914.

Below left: Anonymous: Grigori Rasputin with his children outside the house in which his family lived. Rasputin himself lived in St Petersburg, and only came home to see his family occasionally. Village near the Urals, 1910–1916.

Below right. Anonymous: Rasputin's daughter with a friend, outside the family home. Village near the Urals, 1912–1916.

Above right: Anonymous: Nikolai II in the uniform of an officer of the Preobrashensky regiment. This uniform was worn on ceremonial occasions only. C. 1900.

Below right: Adjutant General V A Dedyulin, commandant of the troops at the court of Nikolai II. He was a close confidant of the Tsar. C. 1900.

Left: Anonymous: Grigori Rasputin, Prince Putyatin and General Lohmann. Petrograd, 1916.

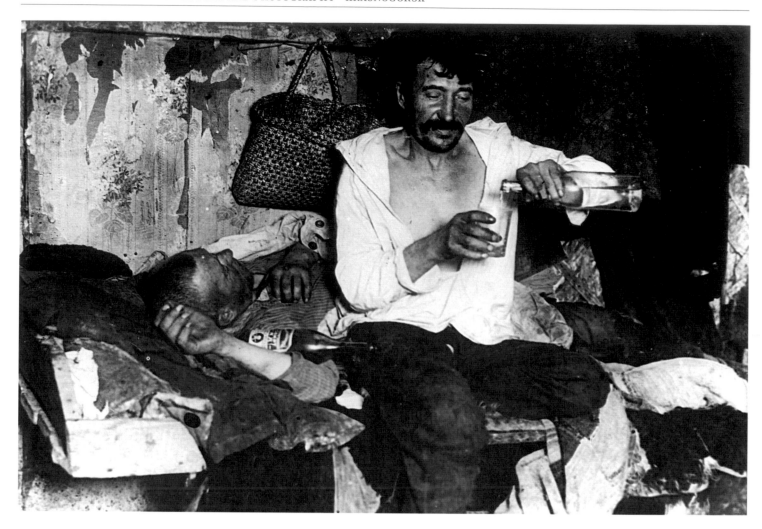

Anonymous: Night shelter in the slums of Moscow. At this time there were a lot of people out of work who sought refuge in places of this kind. Moscow, c. 1904.

Anonymous: Blind bandura player. He is playing this traditional Ukrainian musical instrument to earn money. 1914.

Anonymous: Residents of the night shelter. Moscow, c. 1904.

*Anonymous: Residents of the
night shelter. Moscow, c. 1904.*

*R Dorev: Weekly market at
the banks of the Moscva,
Moscow.*

P A Ocup: Na Krovy temple, from an unknown album. Temples of this kind were built at the scene of murders, as a memorial to the victim. This is where Tsar Alexander II was murdered in 1881. St Petersburg, after 1910.

*Alexander Alexandrovich
Nasvetevich: Building the
memorial to Alexander II in
the Kremlin. From the album
of the amateur photographer
Major-General Alexander
Alexandrovich Nasvetevich.
The memorial was in the inside of the building. It was
destroyed after the October
Revolution like many other
cultural sites. Moscow, 1895.*

*Anonymous: Photographs
from a military album.
1890–1900.*

*Anonymous: Photographs
from a military album.
1890–1900.*

A Renz/F Schrader: Portraits from the album Officers of the Mounted Grenadier Regiment of Guards. *Watercolors by Professor A Scharlemann. Near St Petersburg, 1899.*

A Renz/F Schrader: Portraits from the album Officers of the Mounted Grenadier Regiment of Guards. *Watercolors by Professor A Scharlemann. Near St Petersburg, 1899.*

A Renz/F Schrader: Portraits from the album Officers of the Mounted Grenadier Regiment of Guards. *Watercolors by Professor A Scharlemann. Near St Petersburg, 1899.*

A Renz/F Schrader: Portraits from the album Officers of the Mounted Grenadier Regiment of Guards. *Watercolors by Professor A Scharlemann. Near St Petersburg, 1899.*

Above left: M N Gribov:
Ascent of a captive balloon.
From the album Large-scale
maneuvers at Kursk. *1902.*

Above right: M N Gribov:
Cars on military exercises;
their engines were designed
by the inventor Vassily
W Lushky. From the album
Large-scale maneuvers at
Kursk. *1902.*

Below. P A Ocup: Army
movements with motorized
vehicles. From an album.
1910–1913.

Below: P A Ocup: Army
movements with motorized
vehicles. From an album.
1910–1913.

*Above: Polyakov: Officers'
lunch during military exercises in the village of Ela-
gino, near Moscow. 1885.*

*Below right: Anonymous:
Pilots of the III Airborne
Regiment. Holders of the
Georgy Order. From the
album Episodes on active
service from the life of the
III Airborne Regiment in the
First World War. South-west
front, 1914/15.*

*Right and below: Anony-
mous: Bombs and Molotov
cocktails in an airplane.
From the album Episodes on
active service from the life of
the III Airborne Regiment in
the First World War. South-
west front, 1914/15.*

the flower of the intelligentsia, sits in the marshes for years, sits there on a narrow, hundred-verst-long strip known as the front, sits there—with conviction (is that not a symbol?). Tiny men and an enormous country. ... A little piece of land, the edge of a wood, a clearing, are enough to accommodate the corpses of hundreds of men and horses. In late 1916 the power of the Russian state was overtaken by sickness—this sickness was helped on by the war, which had for three years battered the organism of the state, revealed it in all its fragility and rotten-ness, and sucked out its last creative strength. In the spring of 1916, thirteen million peasants, craftsmen, and other men were swallowed by being called up, and the direct consequence of this was a clogging of the principal arteries that supplied the whole country."

Anonymous: The Russian fleet in the Gulf of Nagasaki. The frigate Pamjat Asova firing a salute on 15 April 1891. From the album The Pacific-Vladivostok Military Fleet. *1891.*

Southwestern command ordered a report on incidents and military movements to be drawn up with the help of a photographer. Unfortunately only two albums have survived of all the documents produced: Number 8, *Battlefields and Positions* and Number 9, already mentioned above, *Life in the Trenches, April 1917.* Each photograph is described with scrupulous accuracy. Unfortunately there is no complete index to the other albums, so we can only speculate about the contents of the lost documents. The title page of album Number 9 looked like this:

Index number 9
Ninth Regiment of Siberian Grenadiers,
Grand Duke Field Marshall Nikolai Nikolayevich

Anonymous: From the album The Pacific-Vladivostok Military Fleet. *With the inscription: "From the officers of the Corvette Naesdnik. 1886–1889". Nagasaki, 1891.*

Above: Anonymous: Soldiers swearing loyalty to the provisional governement on 21 March 1917. From the album Everyday scenes with the 9th Grenadier Regiment Siberia. *South-west front, Lushnetsky district in Volinskaya, 1917.*

Below: Anonymous: Easter presents for soldiers on 2 April 1917.

Photographic Album with everyday scenes 43 pages

Started 10 March 1917
Finished 13 April 1917"

Photographs in this album show the hard life of soldiers and officers. They had to fight in the trenches, and also had to make sure that the re-

giment was fed. Trenches, dugouts, wells—everything was built by the soldiers.

Another series captured an interesting event. On 21 March 1917, the Ninth Regiment of Siberian Grenadiers swore an oath of fidelity to the the new government. On this occasion a prayer of thanksgiving was given, and subsequently the soldiers swore the oath, and kissed the cross, the Bible, and their regimental flag.

Easter was celebrated in the units early in April. One would imagine that it would be difficult to carry out the Easter ceremonial under front-line conditions, but the soldiers found a way: one of the buildings was equipped as a church, a painting of the Redeemer was made, and a choir was selected. The regimental priest, Konstantin Bogoyavlensky, celebrated a solemn service following all the rites of the Orthodox Church.

'Poetry in stone', church architecture, occupies an important place in Russian culture. The imperial family owned an artistically outstanding album called *The New Jerusalem*. It contains pictures of the Voskresyensky Cathedral—lavishly decorated, with unique frescoes on Biblical subjects—and other parts of the monastery complex in Istra. Cathedral and monastery were barbarically destroyed in December 1941 by German soldiers billeted there for twelve days. Today large parts of the monastery are being restored or rebuilt, and the detailed photographs are of considerable use for this operation.

We have only been able to touch on a small proportion of the archive's collection here. The very full collections of photographs in Russian museum archives help us to a better understanding of the people and to see the roots of many contemporary phenomena.

Anonymous: Orchestra of the 9th Grenadier Regiment. On the flag is written: "Long live free Russia and the provisional governement! Unity and victory are needed for the existence of free Russia." South-west front, near Lvov, 1917.

Photographic Processes

DAGUERREOTYPE
(1839 to about 1860)

Two Frenchmen, Joseph Nicéphore Niepce and Louis Jacques Mandé Daguerre, experimented independently on transferring images onto light-sensitive material using the camera obscura. They heard of each other's experiments through their optician, and in 1829 entered into a contract to conduct their research together. After Niepce's death in 1833, Daguerre developed the latent image and succeeded in fixing it. He won François Arago over in 1839, and the latter recommended the French Government to buy the process and present it to the public. People were fascinated by the brilliance and detail of the pictures, and only later realized the disadvantage of being able to produce only a single copy. The process rapidly became popular, in America as well, where it remained the preferred form of photography until the 1860s.

Daguerreotypes required a layer of silver on a copper plate, and this was originally applied by hammering on silver leaf, later by galvanization. The plate was carefully cleaned and polished. The next stage then had to occur within a few minutes, or the cleaning process had to be repeated.

In the early days an exposure of fifteen to thirty minutes was required, later reduced to ten seconds to a minute. The plate was developed in a light-proof wooden box. Its floor consisted of a metal bowl filed with mercury. The plate could be laid at an angle above this. The mercury was warmed with a spirit lamp, the progress of development could be checked through a small window of yellow glass that could be shut. The daguerreotype was then rinsed with alcohol and washed with distilled water before fixative was poured over it. The finished daguerreotype was dried by holding it over an open flame and breathing on the surface until the moisture all evaporated.

CALOTYPE, TALBOTYPE
(1840 to c. 1865)

William Henry Fox Talbot had been working on exposing and fixing an image on paper sensitized with silver chloride in Lacock in England since 1834. Talbot was alarmed by Daguerre's announcements to the public, and introduced his process a few weeks later. This produced a negative, which meant that many copies of a picture could be made.

In 1841 Talbot discovered that he could develop an image that was present in latent form. From this point early photographers worked along two different lines. The negative image was developed, and a positive print made by copying.

The term "calotype" which Talbot introduced for his process in 1841 is reserved for paper negatives and their prints, the details of which are not as sharp as those produced by glass negatives.

In England calotypes (also known as talbotypes) were slow to catch on in comparison with daguerreotypes because Talbot had such a rigid licensing system. It lost significance after about ten years with the introduction of the wet collodion process.

Talbot treated a sheet of good-quality writing paper on one side with silver nitrate solution, then dried it. Light-sensitive halogen silver was produced by soaking in a solution of potassium iodide, and it was then rinsed again and dried in the dark. Sensitivity was enhanced by placing the paper for a short time in a solution Talbot called silver gallonitrate, a mixture of acetic acid, silver nitrate, and gallic acid.

After further rinsing and drying the paper had to be used quickly, as it could be kept for only a few hours. Exposure in the camera obscura took at least a minute in bright sunshine, considerably longer in the early days of the process.

The paper was developed by immersion in the silver gallonitrate solution that has already been mentioned, slightly warmed for the purpose. The appearance of the negative could be observed in red or yellow light in the darkroom. After thorough intermediate rinsing it was fixed, rinsed, and dried in the air.

Herschel had already come up with the idea of using wax to make the negatives transparent in order to shorten copying times and improve definition. Eduard Baldus had further modified the process in order to prevent the image from sinking into the paper felt. After waxing he applied a thin gelatine solution containing iodine salts and exposed the wet, sensitized paper through a glass plate. Similar surface coatings were also made with albumin and collodion.

WET COLLODION PLATE
(1851 to c 1900)

Shortly after the invention of collodion, attempts were made to make use of this quick-drying, clear substance in photography. Frederick S Archer, an Englishman, had the greatest success in this field with a process which caught on rapidly from 1851. Despite the complexities involved in its use, the wet collodion process was considered the best photographic process in the second half of the nineteenth century. It was essential that all stages of the process were carried out faultlessly, so that large photographic studios employed specialists for individual tasks, who then worked together in teams.

At the beginning of the process iodine and bromine salts were added to the collodion, and they later formed the light-sensitive halogen silver in combination with silver nitrate.

The glass plates were carefully chosen and cleaned in several stages: this was as significant for the success of the process as polishing was for the daguerreotype. In order to prevent the skin of collodion from peeling off the plate it was possible to apply an adhesive base of rubber solution, guttapercha, albumin, or gelatine.

The glass plate was held horizontal and the collodion poured onto its center. If it was of the right consistency and the glass was clean, it spread over the surface almost on its own, otherwise it could be assisted by tilting. As the liquid dried very quickly, the procedure was particularly difficult in the case of large plates. Before the coating dried out completely, the photographer plunged the plate into a narrow, upright trough or bowl containing silver nitrate to sensitize it.

Exposure had to take place before the layer began to dry up. It took about five to eight seconds in a studio with bright northern light less than a second in bright sunlight, and several minutes in diffused daylight. Long exposures needed special precautions to prevent the plate from drying out too soon.

One of the many ferrous sulfate solutions was usually used as a developer. The procedure itself was rather like pouring on the collodion, and was continued until the image was sufficiently dark. As the collodion plates were further used to produce copies, they had to have much greater contrast than modern negatives. For this reason the plate was soaked in a reinforcing solution of pyro-gallol and silver nitrate, then fixed and rinsed. To protect the sensitive layer of collodion from mechanical damage, the plate was gently warmed after drying and given a coat of clear varnish.

COLLODION POSITIVE
(1852 to c. 1890)

Frederick Scott Archer, who had introduced his collodion process in London in 1851, also pointed out the possibilty of transforming the dark negative into a whitish image by bleaching it in a solution of mercuric chloride and providing a dark backing. It then looked like a positive. Ambrotype was a simple, cheap process, and soon replaced the daguerreotype. Its period of success came to an end when portrait photography was given a new form in Paris in 1853 by Eugène Disdéri's *carte de visite*. It was still available until 1890, however.

Especially pure collodion was used to keep the shadows clear and dark. A white image was ensured by maximum avoidance of organic substances during sensitization and development.

Exposure time was reduced to half in comparison with the negative process. An image appeared in a very few seconds in the fast-working ferrous-sulfate developer. A potassium cyanide solution was used as fixer.

The coated side of the completed plate could be colored. In this case it was finished off with a protective varnish or covered with a glass plate and painted or backed with a darker color. If color was not used, the coated side could be lacquered directly and the picture viewed from the back.

COLLODION PAPER
(1865–1920)

Good experience with collodion plates allowed George Wharton Simpson, an Englishman, to introduce collodion-coated paper in 1864. Collodion paper kept better, and was three times more sensitive than albumin paper. For these reasons hand-made material that retained its sensitivity for a year came on to the market as early as 1867. It was also the first roll paper, in lengths of up to a kilometer, to be coated industrially from 1885. It was preferred for portraits and photographs of objects by specialist photographers.

Collodion emulsion was prepared from three basic solutions, containing collodion, a salt (lithium or calcium chloride) and silver nitrate, which were poured over baryta paper stretched on a frame. Processing was as for albumin paper. It was also possible simply to copy on to the paper and develop it.

FERROTYPE
(1853 to the 1930s)

Adolphe Alexander Martin changed the material to which the light-sensitive layer was attached from glass to a darkened iron plate. This process was introduced to the public in Paris in 1853. It was cheaper than ever, robust, and complete in a few minutes. It thus met the minimal demands of clients whose favors street photographers—they often had no photographic training—were so eager to gain. The invention of the carte de visite made ferrotypes a little less popular, but that was all. Metal-plate photography survived into the 1930s on festive occasions and in parks and seaside resorts.

The thin plates were lacquered with an asphalt solution to which lampblack or umber was added; it was then thickened by boiling. It was not long before the plates could be bought ready-made. Subsequent processes were similar to those for the ambrotype, though gelatine layers were used in later years.

PHOTOGRAVURE, HELIOGRAVURE
(1880 to the present day)

An early form of this photomechanical printing process had been introduced by Talbot as early as 1858. Photogravure started to be used commercially in a superior version developed by Karel Klisch in Vienna in 1879 and introduced to the public in 1886.

Ink for photogravure printing is held in tiny indentations in a metal plate. These are produced by irregular distribution of asphalt dust, making the structure of the tonal values look different from the even pattern of other printing processes.

Art photographers used it as a high-class printing process for small runs, but photogravure was also ideal for reproducing other kinds of works of art. The magazine *Camera Work* (1903–1917), published by Alfred Stieglitz, is an outstanding example of this.

The copper plate was carefully cleaned, then placed in a box and treated with a thin layer of asphalt dust which was later melted by heating the plate. This produced an irregular pattern which made it possible to reproduce half-tones. On this a negative pigment print was developed, and this and the asphalt layer served to resist corrosion. The back and non-printing parts were covered with asphalt paint and the plate was etched in a concentrated solution of ferric chloride, then cleaned, degreased and polished.

For printing the plate was warmed, photogravure ink rubbed on with the ball of the thumb or a tampon and then wiped clean again. The ink was now only in the indentations etched into the copper plate and was transferred to moistened photogravure paper by a photogravure press.

GELATINE PLATE AND FILM
(1878 to the present)

Richard Leach Maddox, an Englishman, invented the dry gelatine plate. He stopped working with collodion, partly because of problems with his own health and continued experiments which had already been abandoned with gelatine as a bonding agent for bromyrite. He published details of his process in 1871.

The manufacture of dry gelatine plates was almost exclusively restricted to industrial operations because of heavy technological requirements and highly restricted production tolerances. The wet collodion process had already reached a high standard which did not permit general introduction of the dry gelatine plate until the process had gone beyond the experimental stage and the plates could be produced in large quantities at acceptable prices. The advantages of the dry gelatine plate over the wet collodion process were its considerably greater sensitivity, which made problem-free snapshots available for the first time. The ease of processing, and the fact that the plate would keep for several years if necessary. This cleared the way for amateur photography.

The greater sensitivity had many causes. One of these was that gelatine when used as a binding agent for silver salts itself enhanced sensitivity. Also silver iodide was being replaced by silver bromide, which is much more sensitive to light. The silver salts were not produced by subsequent "silvering", but at the same time as the emulsion. But the clinching feature was the enormous increase in sensitivity caused by warming, boiling or ammonia-treating of the emulsion before coating: the so-called "ripening" process. Sensitivity was up to eighty times that of a wet collodion plate. After cooling and setting, the emulsion was pushed through a sieve in noodle shape and washed in cold water to remove all soluble constituents. The emulsion was liquefied again by warming it up then pouring it onto thoroughly cleaned glass plates. The dried plates were cut to the format required.

Processing was at first not without its problems, as darkrooms and camera equipment were seldom suitable for the unusual degree of sensitivity without some modification. Working in very dim red light or complete darkness or with very fast shutters soon became the norm, however. The collodion plate survived only in reproduction technology and astronomical photography.

Bibliography

Literature

The most significant books consulted by the authors:

Chistyakova, A V : *Rabota V V Stasova s chitatelyami Otdelenya iskusstv Publichnoi biblioteki.* Trudy Gosudarstvennoi Publichnoi biblioteki im. M E Saltykova-Shchedrina (*The Work of V V Stasov with the Readers of the Art Departement of the Public Library.* In: Works of the Public Library M E Saltykov-Shchedrin), Leningrad 1957

Chibisov, K V : *Ocherki po istorii fotografii (Reports on the History of Photography)*, Moscow 1987

Golovina, A A : *Letopisec revolyucii. K 100-letiyu so dnya roshdenya V K Bully.* In: Sovetskoe foto (*Chronicler of the Revolution. For the Hundredth Birthday of V K Bulla.* In: Soviet Photo), Moscow 1983

Gosudarstvennye arhivy RSFSR: *Spavochnik-putevoditel* (State Archives of the USSR: *Reference Books*), Moscow 1980

Jzobretenya i usovershenstvovanya, sdelannye po fotografii J V Boldyrevym (Inventions and Improvements after Photographs of I V Boldyrev), St Petersburg 1883

Kalenichenko, A S : *Obzor fotodokumentov P S Chukova*, hranyashchihsya v LGAKFFD (*Summary of the Photographic Documents of P S Shukov,* kept in the State Archive for Film- and Photodocuments), Leningrad 1971

Kalenichenko, A S : *Obzor fotodokumentov semi fotografov Bully,* hranyashchsya v LGAKFFD (*Summary of the Photographic Documents of the Photographer Family Bulla,* kept in the State Archive for Film- and Photodocuments), Leningrad 1983

Morozov S : *Russkaya hudoshestvennaya fotografiya.* Ocherki po istorii fotografii 1839–1917 (*Russian Art-Photography,* Essays on the History of Photography 1839–1917), Moscow 1961

Morozov S : *Russkie puteshestvenniki fotografy (Russian Travel-Photography)*, Moscow 1953

Morozov S : *Tvorcheskaya fotografiya (Creativ Photography)*, Moscow 1986

Stasov, V V : *Fotografiya i gravjura.* Sobranie sochinenij V V Stasova (V V Stasov: *Photography and Copperplates.* Complete Edition of his Works, v. 1), St Petersburg 1894

Ukazatel fotograficheskoy vystavki, ustroennoj lyubitelyami etogo iskusstva (Inventory of the Photo Exhibition, organized by the Enthusiasts of this Art), St Petersburg 1888

Photojournals and Newspapers

Fotograf (The Photographer), 1880–1884

Fotograf (The Photographer), St Petersburg 1864–1866, edited by Alexander V Fribes

Fotograf-Lyubitel (The Amateur Photographer), 1890–1909, edited by Adrian M Lavrov, since the end of 1900 by S M Prokudin-Gorsky

Fotograf-Praktik (The Photo-Practitioner), 1907–1908

Fotograficheskaya illustraciyu (The Photographic Illustration), Tver 1863

Fotograficheskie novosti (Photographic News), St Petersburg 1907–1918, edited by the commercial firm of I Steffen

Fotograficheskij listok (The Photographic Newspaper), St Petersburg 1906–1917, edited by the commercial firm of J Jochim

Fotograficheskiy vestnik (The Photographic Messenger), 1867, edited by G Vogel

Fotograficheskiy vestnik (The Photographic Messenger), St Petersburg 1887–1911, edited by Pavel M Olchin

Fotograficheskoe obozrenye (The Photographic Review), 1896–1903

Fotograficheskoe obozrenye (The Photographic Review), St Petersburg 1865–1870, edited by Alexander V Fribes

Moskovskie vedomosti (Moscow Reports)

Novoe vremja (New Time)

Obzor graficheskih iskusstv (Review of the Graphic Arts), 1878–1885

Promyshlenost (The Economy)

Russkaya Mysl (The Russian Thought)

Russkij fotograficheskiy vestnik (The Russian Photographic Messenger), 1915–1916

Russkiy fotograficheskiy Churnal (The Russian Photographic Journal), Odessa 1895–1898, edited by L E Mikhailov-Muchkin

Russkoe slovo (The Russian Word)

Svet (The Light), 1877–1878

Svetopis (Light-Painting), 1858–1859

Vestnik fotografii (The Messenger of Photography), Moscow 1908–1918

Vsya Rossiya (Whole Russia), 1904–1908

Zvestiya russkogo obshchestva Lyubiteley fotografii (News of the Russian Society for the Amateurs of Photography), 1903–1907

Index

Figures in normal type refer to the text, those in italics to photographs.

Abadi, Martin 40, *45*, *48*
Abamelek-Lasarev 18
Adrianov 22
Akhatov, S T 47
Alexander II 51, *241*, *242*
Alexander III *230*, *232*
Alexandrovna, Tsarina Maria *106*, *198*
Anderson, K *109*
Andreyev, V V 182
Andreyev-Burlak, V H 142
Asikritov, D *159*
Ayvazovsky, Ivan Konstantinovich 18

Bakhrushin, A P 24, 38, 50
Bakhrushin, V A 28
Bakst, Léon (Lev Samuilovich Rosenberg) 28
Barash, P R 148
Barshevsky, Ivan Fyodorovich 20
Barushin *50*
Batenkov, S G 47
Begrov, Alexander Karlovich 20, *49*
Belyavsky, M 140
Benois, Alexander Nikolayevich 20, 28, 109
Bergamasco, Charles 10, 16, 102, *106*, 132–134, *134*, *135*, *137*, *139*
Bergner, Karl August *39*, 47, *52*, *53*
Bernhard, A *107*, *140*
Bernhardt, Sarah *140*
Biardo, Polina 38
Birkin, Dmitri Gavrilovich 15
Blanquart-Evrard, Louis Désiré 10
Blok, Alexander Alexandrovich 150, 182, 213
Blumenthal, A G 148
Bobrinsky, Aleksei count 101
Bobrinsky, Alexander count 101
Bobrinsky, family 100
Bobrinsky, Vladimir count 101, *101*, 102
Bodarevsky, N K *49*
Bogoyavlensky, Konstantin 252
Boldyrev, Ivan Vasilyevich *14*, 15, *16*, 18, 75, *76*, *78–80*, 81
Borhard, Richard 10
Botkin, Mikhail Pyotrovich 75, *80*, 150

Brandel, Konrad 18
Bruni, Fyodor Antonovich 18
Bucharin, Nikolai Ivanovich *228*
Bukar, Mikhail 51, *61–65*
Bulla, Alexander Karlovich 172, 182, *182*
Bulla, Karl Karlovich 7, 32, 35, *94*, *96–99*, 109, 111, *119*, *120*, 121, *124–129*, *132*, 140, *143*, *145*, 172, 174, 175, 182, *182–185*, 212
Bulla, Viktor Karlovich 172, 182, *182*, 184, *184*, 186
Bunin, Ivan A 157
Byling, B 25
Bystrov, D 140

Chapakovsky, Alexander Ilyich 10
Chebyshev, Pafnuty Lvovich 148
Chegolev 30
Chekhov, Anton Pavlovich *149*, 150–152, *152*, 156, *156*, 157, *157*, 159, *159*, 160, *160*
Chekhov, family *149*, *152*
Chekhov, Mikhail Pavlovich 151
Chekhova, Maria Pavlovna 150, 157, 159
Cherbina, Nikolai Fyodorovich 38, *41*
Cheremetyev 100
Chertkov, Alexander D 38, 47
Chertkov, Vladimir Grigorevich 38, 47, 152
Chevchenko, Taras Grigoryevich 102
Chevreuil 20
Chishkin, Ivan Ivanovich 20, *49*
Chitsherin, V 156
Chomyakov, Aleksei Stepanovich 38, *49*
Chuvalov 100
Chyukin, Pyotr Ivanovich 48, 50
Courbet, Gustave 24

Daguerre, Louis Jacques Mandé 7–9, 12, 19, 28, 148, 149
Dashkova, princess *107*
Davidson 25
Davignon, Alfred 40, *46*, 47
Dedyulin, V A *235*
Demchinsky 23
Dementyev, Pavel Matveyevich 22
Denier, Andrei I 7, 9, 10, 15, 40, 46, 47, *49*, *51*, 101, 102, *107*, 132, 133, *133*, 134, *141*
Dmitriev, Maksim Pyotrovich 19, 20, 24, 25, 27, *67*, 74, 121, *142*, 212, 213, *213*, 214
Dolina, M I *138*, 142
Dorev, R *240*

Dossekin, V 10, *117*
Dostoyevsky, Fyodor Mikhailovich 150
Drenteln 150
Drushinin, Alexander Vasilyevich 46, *147*, 149, 150
Dubovsky, Nikolai Nikolayevich *49*
Dumas, J 149

Eastman, George 15, 24
Ernuf 12
Ertel, Alexander Ivanovich 150

Fedorovna, Tzarin Alexandra 121, *230*
Fedotov, Andrei Shdanovich 150
Fedotova, Glikeriya N 160
Felisch, Albert Eduard 22
Fischer, K 25, 140
Freiwirt 22
Fribes, Alexander Vikentevich 9, 10, 12
Fried, G *204*, *205*, *207–210*
Fritsche, J F 7, 8

Garnovsky, N T 38
Ge, Nikolai Nikolayevich 12
Geld, baron von 10
Germagis 15
Gippius, Sinaida *141*
Glazunov, Alexander Konstantinovich 182
Glinka, G N *138*, *152*
Gogol, Nikolai Vasilyevich 8, 101, 149
Golitsyn, M N 148
Goncharov, Ivan Alexandrovich 149
Gorky, Maksim *157*, 182
Gorskaya, R *132*
Gratl, F 25
Grdlicke 25
Grekov, Aleksei Fyodorovich 8
Greym, M *116*, 117
Gribov, I I 120
Gribov, M N *249*
Grigorevich, Dimitri Vasilyevich 46, 149, 150
Grinzburg, I J 84
Grum-Grshimailo, Grigori Yefimovich 18
Gudin *114*

Hahn, C E *95*, 213, *218–225*, *231*, *233*
Hammel, I H 7
Herzen, Alexander Ivanovich 38, 46, *47*

Hopewood, Sam 72

Isaakovich, S S *149*
Ivanitsky, A M 140
Ivanitsky, K 25
Ivanov, Alexander Andreyevich *146*, 149
Ivanov, Mikhail 148
Ivanov-Terentev, A A 33

Jochim, commercial firm 31
Jordan, Friedrich Ludwig *146*, 149

Kamensky 150
Karelin, Andrei Andreyevich 23, 27, *54–57*, 212
Karelin, Andrei Osipovich 15–17, 19, 48, 50, 212
Karelin, family *54*
Karelina, Olga Grigoryevna *54*
Karpov, Ilya Ivanovich 22
Karrik, Vladimir Andreyevich 12, 13, 81, *84*
Kerensky, Alexander *98*
Kessler 230
Ketcher, N Ch 38
Kirchner, Otto *168, 169*
Kirilov, G K 142
Kiselev, A A *49*
Komissarshevskaya, Vera Fyodorovna 135, *137*, 141, 142, *142, 143*
Komissarshevsky, F *142*
Kordynov 23
Kordysh, Yosif 51, *58–60*
Korolenko, Vladimir Galaktionovich *55*, 150
Korsh 47
Koslovsky, V *88, 89*
Kotelov, I 25
Kovalevsky, E P 149, 150
Kovalsky, I *232*
Kozlov 23
Kramskoy, Ivan Nikolayevich 12, 47, 48, 134
Krashkovsky, Yosif Yevtafevich 12
Krzesinska, M F 135
Kuindshi, Archip Ivanovich *49*, 134
Kulibin, Nikolai 12
Kulshenko, Stefan Vasilyevich 30
Kuprin, Alexander Ivanovich *145*
Kuznetsov, N D *49*, 74

Lagorio, Lev Feliksovich 12
Laptev, S D 15
Lasareva, Comtess *71*
Lavrov, Adrian Mikhailovich 20, 22–24
Lavrovskaya *137*
Levashov 100, 109, *115*
Levenson, T 34
Levitsky, Sergei Lvovich 7–10, 17, 46, 47, *48, 50, 51*, 101, 102, *103*, 132, 134, *137, 146, 147*, 149, 150
Liadov, K *141*
Lippmann, Gabriele 25
Lobovikov, Sergei A 30, 33, 212
Lohmann, General *235*

Lopuchina-Demidova, comtess *109*
Lorens, A 111, *121*, 132, 134, *137*
Lumière, brothers 27
Lushsky, Vasili W *159*, 160

Maksimov, V N *49*
Mamin-Sibiryak, Dimitri Narkisovich 150
Mamontov, family *39*, 47
Mamontov, Savva Ivanovich *39, 52, 229*
Mamovsky, V E *49*
Mankov, van 9
Markevich 150
Masalitinov 23
Maykov 46
Mazurin, Aleksei Sergeyevich *2, 51, 60*
Melodiev, I E 35
Mendeleev, Dmitri Ivanovich 12, 17
Metz, G. G. de 30
Mey, Albert Ivanovich 160, *161–166*
Mikhailov, Georgi 36
Mikhailovich, A 22
Mikhailovich-Mushkin, L I 36
Mroshenko, M A *49*
Mrozovskaya, Yelena *138*, 140–142, *158*
Mücke, Eduard Wilhelm 147
Münster, A 48
Muravyev-Apostol, M I 47
Muravyev-Karsky, N M 47
Murzin, F Nikolayevich 33
Musatov, P 12

Nadar 20
Naprovnik, E *141*
Nastyukov, Mikhail P 19, *109–111*
Nasvetevich, Alexander Alexandrovich *242*
Nekrasov, N A 149
Nemirovich-Danshenko, Vladimir Ivanovich 159
Nevsky, Alexander 109
Nielsen, W 25
Niepce de Saint-Victor, Claude Marie François 10, 12
Nikolai II 26, 35, *198*, 225, 230, 231, *233, 235*
Nikolayevna, Maria *104*
Nistrem, K 148
Nordman, Natalya *69, 70*
Nostits, Ivan Grigorevich count 20, 24

Ocup, P. A 140, *241, 249*
Okulovsky 10
Olchin, Pavel Matveyevich 18
Opitz, F *158*
Orlov, Pimen Nikitich *146*, 149
Ostrovsky, P 46, *75*, 149
Ovalyani, Prince *70*

Panayev, Ivan Ivanovich 9, 10
Panayout, brothers 25
Panina, S V 156
Pasetti, K A *142*
Pavlenkov, Florenti Fyodorovich 7, 10
Pavlov, Ivan Petrovich 75

Pavlov, P P *159*
Pavlova, Anna Pavlovna 135, 182
Pavlovna, grand duchesse Maria *92, 93*
Pavlovsky, I I *153–155*
Perl, G 140
Petipa, Maria Mariusovna *135*
Petrov, Nikolai Alexandrovich 30–33, 36
Petrov, V 120
Pikkel, I *141*
Pisaemsky 46
Platonova, I *137*
Podgorny, N A *158*
Poechin 46
Polonsky, Yakov 46, *54*
Polyakov 212, *250*
Pozen, L V *49*
Prileshaev, A I 36
Prokudin-Gorsky, S M 29, 30, 36
Pushchin, I I 48
Pushkin, Alexander *95*, 102
Putyatin, count *235*

Radetsky, S 149
Radishchev *66*
Raoult, Ivan Pyotrovich *11*
Rasputin, family *234*
Rasputin, Grigori *94, 234, 235*
Renz, A 140, *245–248*
Repin, Ilya Yefimovich *32, 49, 69, 145*, 182, *215*
Reym, M O 20
Rimski-Korsakov, Nikolai Andreyevich 84
Romanov, House of 9, *196–199*
Ropet, I P 74

Sabelin, I E 38
Sakharov, assessor 147
Samarin, J F 47
Samarova, Maria A 160
Satin, N M 47, 150
Savadsky, Aleksei Karlovich 51, *73*
Savina, M G *132*
Savitsky, N A *49*
Savrasov, S N 33
Scherer und Nabgolz 109
Scherling, M A *144, 145*
Schnaus 10
Schrader, F 140, *245–248*
Schuchardt 10
Semenova, M M 142
Semevsky, M I 46
Semiradsky, Genrich Ippolitovich 20
Semyowsky 46
Senger, Bruno 22
Serbinov, J I 25
Seregin, Profiri Yovovich 151
Sergeyenko, Pyotr Alekseyevich 156, *156*
Shalyapin, Fyodor Ivanovich 142, *144*, *145*, 182
Shapiro, Konstantin 140, *141*, 172
Shcherbak, A V *152*
Shipkina-Kubernik, T 157
Shishkin, Ivan Ivanovich 20, *49*
Shukov, Pavel Semenovich 172

Shuravlev   24
Simonenko, P   10
Skamoni, Georgi Nikolayevich   10
Skassi, A   140
Slakosov, brothers   *42*
Slavina, M   *134*
Solodnikov   148
Solovatov   *214*
Solovev, G S   16, 18, *140*
Somov, Konstantin Andreyevich   28
Sredin, Leonid Valentinovich   *157, 160*
Sreznevsky, Vyacheslav Izmailovich   12 18, 22, 32, 34
Stanislavsky, Konstantin S   159
Stasov, V V   *6*, 50, 74, 75, *76*, 81, 83, 212
Steffen, commercial firm   22
Steinberg, Yakov Vladimirovich   140, 170, 172
Stroganov   100
Suchachev   23
Suskipi   *109*
Suvorin, Aleksei Sergeyevich   152
Svishov-Paola, Nikolai Ivanovich   33, *228, 229*
Svoev   150
Sytin   27

Talbot, William Henry Fox   7, 8, 12, 19
Temerin, colonel   8
Timiryasev, W   25
Timm, W   48
Tolkachev, A I   22
Tolstaya, Alexandra Lvovna   *185*
Tolstaya, Maria Nikolayevna   *147,* 148
Tolstaya, Sofya Andreyevna   *129,* 152, 156, *156*
Tolstoy, family   *129*
Tolstoy, Lev Nikolayevich   18, 46, *128, 140, 147,* 149, 150, 152, 156, *156,* 157, 182, *184, 185*
Ton, K A   109
Trapani, Anatoli N   33
Tretyakov, Pavel Mikhailovich   47
Trubetsky, S P   47
Tsurikova, Yekaterina Alexandrovna   150
Tulinov, Mikhail Borisovich   150
Turgenev, Ivan Sergeyevich   38, 47, 149
Tyutchev, Fyodor Ivanovich   102, 150

Urusov, A I count   27

Varnerke, Lev Vikentevich   13, 14, 18
Vasilev, A   22, *117,* 213, *216, 217*
Vasnetsov, V   *49*
Vereshagina, S   *117*
Vishnevsky, A L   *83*
Vishnyakov, Yevgeni Petrovich   18, 20
Vladimirsky   20, 22
Vladsky, A   *111–113,* 114
Vogels, Hermann Wilhelm   12
Volkonskaya, Maria Nikolayevna   38, *47*
Volkonskaya, S   *107*
Volkonsky, Sergei Grigorevich   38, 40, *46, 50*
Volkov, Yefim Yefimovich   *49*

Volynsky, A   *141*
Vysotsky, Vladimir   *114*

Weinger, I   101
Werner, A   25
Wesenberg   140
Wilhelm II, Kaiser   *230*

Yemelyanov   *86*
Yermakov, Dmitri Ivanovich   *21, 25,* 51, *60,* 70, 71
Yermolova, Maria N   132
Yershemsky, Alexander Konstantinovich   20, 22
Yurier, I M   135
Yurkovsky, S A   81
Yusupov   100

Zishi, Mikhail Alexandrovich   12

Rear Endpaper
St Petersburg decorated for
its two-hundredth birthday
(see also front endpaper).